The Nicene Creed

*The nature of Christian unity
and the meaning of gospel words*

Edited by
**Mark Gilbert and
Leonardo De Chirico**

❦**matthiasmedia**
SYDNEY · YOUNGSTOWN

Matthias Media
(St Matthias Press Ltd ACN 067 558 365)
Email: info@matthiasmedia.com.au
Internet: matthiasmedia.com.au
Please visit our website for current postal and telephone contact information.

Matthias Media (USA)
Email: sales@matthiasmedia.com
Internet: matthiasmedia.com
Please visit our website for current postal and telephone contact information.

All websites cited in this book were accessed on 20 June 2024.

ISBN 978 1 922980 39 7

Cover design by Carol Lam.
Typesetting by Lankshear Design.

CONTENTS

INTRODUCTION

Leonardo De Chirico and Mark Gilbert
(editors)

Can evangelicals and Roman Catholics confess the Nicene Creed together?

Is it loving to appear united when we are not? This is the question we need to ask in the year 2025, as we mark the 1700th anniversary of the Council of Nicaea, the first council of the whole Christian church (after that of Jerusalem, spoken of in Acts 15).

This occasion will prompt many initiatives aimed at celebrating the Nicene Creed, which was a key outcome of the council. Many of these initiatives will have an ecumenical agenda based on the appropriation of the creed as a sign and instrument of Christian unity among evangelicals and Roman Catholics (among others). In Pope Francis's words:

> The Council of Nicaea was a milestone in the Church's history. The celebration of its anniversary invites Christians to join in a hymn of praise and thanksgiving to the Blessed Trinity and in

particular to Jesus Christ, the Son of God, "consubstantial with the Father", who revealed to us that mystery of love. At the same time, Nicaea represents a summons to all Churches and Ecclesial Communities to persevere on the path to visible unity and in the quest of fitting ways to respond fully to the prayer of Jesus "that they may all be one. As you, Father, are in me and I am in you, may they also be in us, so that the world may believe that you have sent me" (Jn 17:21).[1]

It's often argued that the Nicene Creed is an important basis for achieving greater unity among evangelicals and Catholics because we share a high view of the creed and consider it a foundational summary of our faiths. The assumption behind the argument is that evangelicals and Catholics share the faith expressed in the Creed (including, for example, the doctrines of the Trinity, Christ, the Holy Spirit, salvation and the church). If that is true, we can indeed use this 1700th anniversary as an opportunity to deepen our unity.

This book will respectfully challenge that assumption. Our goal is not to deny what is in common, but to ask questions about its depth, given the fundamental differences that evangelicals and Catholics express and that give rise to different accounts of the gospel. While evangelicals and Catholics can join voices in professing the

---

1 Pope Francis, 'Spes Non Confundit: Bull of Indiction of the Ordinary Jubilee of the Year 2025', *The Holy See* (www.vatican.va/content/francesco/en/bulls/documents/20240509_spes-non-confundit_bolla-giubileo2025.html).

Nicene Creed, does it mean they can do so *theologically*? Do we mean the same things by the words we are saying? And is the Nicene Creed a sufficient basis for unity?

To answer these questions, we'll look closely at each article of the Nicene Creed. Each chapter will aim to:

1. appreciate what that article testifies to in our Christian faith
2. show how evangelicals and Roman Catholics have applied that article in the development of their doctrine and practice, and
3. show where the Roman Catholic Church has taken the meaning of that article beyond biblical teaching.

Before we look at specific articles, this book will begin with a grounding in the historical context of the creed, followed by the creed's foundation in the Protestant principle of *sola scriptura*. We'll then move to look at the creed's trinitarian framework.

After looking through each element of the creed, from the person and work of Jesus to the life in the world to come, we'll answer the very significant question of whether the creed is sufficient as a shared basis for meaningful Christian belief, confession, fellowship and ministry. To do this we will look briefly at two doctrines that are so important to evangelicals but that are not found in the Nicene Creed.

In doing this, we hope this book will serve the cause of true unity based on the truth of the Scriptures. It will encourage us all to be discerning, and to be wary of the possible dangers of a simplistic and superficial use of the Nicene Creed in our time.

Each of this book's contributors has presented papers at the Rome Scholars and Leaders Network (RSLN), an annual seminar sponsored by the Reformanda Initiative. The Reformanda Initiative exists to identify, unite, equip and resource evangelical leaders to understand Roman Catholic theology and practice, to educate the evangelical church, and to communicate the gospel. The book originated at the 2023 RSLN seminar and is the fruit of a growing community of evangelical scholars supporting the initiative.

The contributors identify as evangelicals. We understand evangelicalism as the stream of biblical Christianity that affirms the Nicene Creed and that regained momentum at the Protestant Reformation (and subsequent evangelical revivals). While it expresses itself in multiple church traditions, the commitment to the Bible as the supreme authority and to salvation by faith alone distinguishes evangelicalism from Roman Catholicism. Because of its close connections to Reformation Christianity, the book will use the terms 'Protestant' and 'evangelical' interchangeably, in contrast to Roman Catholicism.

Christian unity must always be built on biblical truth —the truth that the Council of Nicaea tried to honour, even in the complexities of history. What Nicaea stood for is necessary to foster unity. This is why it is important to ask what different Christian traditions mean when they profess the Nicene Creed and whether using the same language amounts to a profession of the same faith. It is love that prompts our question, because love must be founded on the truth (Eph 4:15).

1
THE HISTORY OF
THE NICENE CREED
Rachel Ciano

The Nicene Creed has become a symbol of unity in faith communities that speak of Jesus, and it has a long and rich history. The story of its creation takes us back to the early church and the theological controversies that it faced. Ultimately, the Nicene Creed was a response to Arianism—a theologically incorrect and dangerous teaching that insisted that Jesus was not the eternal Son of God, but rather a creature in the created order. In trying to protect the idea of God's oneness, Arius and his followers denied Jesus' rightful place in the Trinity as God the Son. In this chapter we'll explore this story of the Nicene Creed and get a sense of the rich theological history that we have inherited from the early church. This context will help us as we explore each idea in the creed in the following chapters.

The world of Nicaea: the church in the Roman Empire

The fourth-century Roman Empire was a tumultuous time and place, particularly for Christians. For the previous three centuries or so, many of the challenges that the fledgling Christian movement faced came from outside the church. To be a Christian was unpopular, suspect and could even make you an enemy of the state. Many Christians were persecuted and paid a price for their faith, losing their possessions, property and even their lives.

In these first three centuries, there were also challenges inside the church in the form of off-centre teaching, particularly about the nature of Jesus Christ. For example, some belief systems cast Jesus as a sort of spiritual guru who had the spiritual keys to help the spiritual traveller unlock heavenly realms and travel through them to salvation. This teaching, called Gnosticism, understood salvation as attaining special knowledge (or 'gnosis'). Other belief systems wrestled with the question of how Jesus could be both God and man, and sometimes settled on the answer that Jesus only *appeared* to be a human being. This became known as Docetism (from the Greek *dokeo*, meaning 'to seem' or 'to appear').

The growing church responded to these theological challenges in a number of ways. First, it appealed to the authority of apostolic teaching that handed down the teachings of Jesus. Second, it convened local and provincial church gatherings, or councils, to determine the biblical course of action. Third, it constructed 'creeds' (from the Latin, 'I believe') to summarize teaching that followers of Jesus could confess together and learn off by heart. Creeds were often used in preparation for baptism so that baptism candidates clearly understood the meaning of their public faith declaration.

So when it came to addressing Arianism, it was already an established practice for the church to gather its leaders in order to carefully consider what the Scriptures said on a particular issue and form a statement of faith and agreement. Something unprecedented, however, was *who* was to call the Council of Nicaea.

A significant shift in the fourth century was that, for the first time, a Roman emperor was favourable towards Christians. Constantine I claimed to have experienced a conversion to Christianity on the eve of an important battle in 312 AD and, after winning the battle, he attributed the victory to Christ. The following year, he issued a decree that Christianity was to be tolerated across the empire, which was a huge departure from his predecessors.

While the authenticity of Constantine's faith is often debated, there's little doubt that he saw Christianity as the glue that could help bind together the vast, multi-faceted empire; he hoped the church would unite disparate peoples and lands. So when he got wind of disunity *within* the church in the form of theological controversy, it was he who convened the Council of Nicaea in 325 AD to sort it out.

Constantine was ultimately a head of state, not a theologian. As the head of state, he believed he had the right to oversee church issues. Importantly, he had the power to summon church leaders to Nicaea (in today's Türkiye), close to the imperial residence. Constantine helped to cover the travel costs of delegate bishops, many of whom remembered the persecution of previous emperors.

The state was now involved in a process that had previously been the domain of the church alone. As we'll see, in its pursuit of unity, the state ultimately brought about an agreement that was paper thin. This would contribute to the cracks in the apparent unity, which appeared soon after the council. Before we consider how and why that happened, let's consider the nature of the disunity that prompted the council in the first place.

What was all the fuss about?

Welcome onto the stage Arius of Alexandria. Arius' teachings about the nature of Christ were emerging around 318 AD, around the time that Constantine had his conversion experience. Arius was from Alexandria, in the North-African part of the Roman Empire. Arius was trying to figure out the exact nature of Jesus, and particularly his relationship to God the Father. The early Christians had continued to uphold the Jewish teaching that God is one (Deut 6:4). Yet they also held to the teaching that Jesus is God (Phil 2:6; Col 1:15–19) and confessed the Holy Spirit as God (Matt 28:19; Acts 5:3–4; Ps 139:7–8; 1 Cor 2:10–11, 3:16). But what did all this mean? Up to this point, the early church had not yet clearly articulated how these truths held together.

Arius desired to protect the confession of God's unity, oneness and transcendence and did not want to conceive of change in the essence of God. In trying to protect these theological truths, Arius ended up teaching that while God the Father was eternal, Jesus was not; he had a beginning. This made the Son a creature, one who was of a higher order than humankind but of a lower order than God. The Son was capable of change, whereas God was not. Arius' theology maintained that it was Jesus' obedience that led to his adoption into the Godhead, and therefore that salvation for humankind was a result of imitating Jesus' obedience. By this teaching, salvation by grace through faith in the atoning work of the incarnate Son was obliterated.

Rather than seeing the term 'Son' as a description of the relationship between the Father and the Son, Arius saw it as a temporal idea. If no earthly son can be as old as his earthly father, then logically when it comes to God, the Son could not be as old as the Father. Therefore, the Son must be a created being—certainly the greatest created being, but still created and therefore not God the Creator and not equal to God the Father. 'Son' therefore became a metaphor, a term of honour, used to demonstrate that the Son was above all other creatures, even as he was lesser than God.

Arius put it this way, in a letter to his supporter Eusebius, Bishop of Nicomedia:[1]

---

1 This Eusebius is not to be confused with the Eusebius who wrote the first account of the church's history around this time, although he also features in this story.

We are persecuted because we say, 'the Son had a beginning, but God is without beginning' … and, likewise, because we say that he is from nothing. And this we say, because he is neither part of God, nor of any lower essence.[2]

Though Arius himself may have never used this particular wording, the most common summary of his teaching is that *there was a time when the Son was not.* Socrates, a contemporary of Arius, characterized Arius' teaching this way:

"If", said [Arius], "the Father begat the Son, he that was begotten has a beginning of essence; and from this it is evident, that there was when the Son was not."[3]

If Arius was correct, then it meant that Christians, in ascribing deity to Christ, had two Gods.

Paper-thin unity: the Council of Nicaea

Prior to Nicaea, church councils had only been local or provincial in scope. Nicaea was the first empire-wide gathering, featuring representatives from diverse

2 'The Letter of Arius to Eusebius, Bishop of Nicomedia' in P Schaff (ed), *Nicene and Post-Nicene Fathers*, series 2, vol 3, Christian Classics Ethereal Library, p 87 (bishoysblog.com/wp-content/uploads/2015/01/nicene-post-nicene-fathers-series-2-volume-3.pdf).

3 Socrates, *Ecclesiastical History* (c. 318 AD), book 1, chapter 5, in P Schaff (ed), *Nicene and Post-Nicene Fathers*, series 2, vol 2, Christian Classics Ethereal Library, p 28 (ccel.org/ccel/s/schaff/npnf202/cache/npnf202.pdf).

parts of the Roman Empire and the growing church.[4] The council signalled Constantine's movement into the heart of the church, as he sought to exert control to achieve unity. While there were other items on the agenda of the council, the hot topic was Arius' teaching.

There were three broad groups at Nicaea. First, there were the pro-Arians, a fairly small group of about 15. They were led by Eusebius of Nicomedia, because Arius himself was not a bishop and therefore not a member of the council.

Second, there were the anti-Arians. They maintained that the Son was of 'identical essence' to—or *homoousios* with—the Father; after the council, the theologian Athanasius led this cohort.[5]

The third group was the largest and the most disinterested group. They were led by church historian Eusebius of Caesarea who had more than a little soft spot for Emperor Constantine. This group rejected out of hand the idea that Jesus was created and was happy to admit that the Son was begotten of the Father before all time—that is, eternal. Eusebius did, however, reject the idea that Jesus was the same essence as the Father, and instead argued that he was of a *similar* essence to—or *homoiousios* with—the Father.

The battle therefore became over an iota (literally, an 'i'): would the church adopt *homoousios* (of the *same*

---

4 In this way, the Nicaean Council set a significant precedent in church history: the convening of ecumenical councils became the established pattern for dealing with the theological controversies of the day.

5 '*Homoousios*' comes from the combination of '*homo*'—which means 'same'—and '*ousios*'—which means 'essence' or 'nature'.

nature as the Father) or *homoiousios* (of *like nature* as the Father) as their understanding of the Son's nature?

The council decided they were *against* Arianism, but they had more difficulty deciding what they were *for* on this theological question. Many bishops had hesitations because they did not see the term *homoousios* in the Bible, but Constantine exerted pressure which resulted in all but two council members signing off on the Nicene Creed. This exerted pressure, however, created a forced unity, and there was not necessarily a shared agreement on the meaning of the words chosen.

The Creed of Nicaea: one iota of difference

Here is the creed as it appeared in 325 AD, which comes from a letter Eusebius of Caesarea wrote to his church:[6]

> We believe in One God, the Father, Almighty, Maker of all things visible and invisible:
>
> And in One Lord Jesus Christ, the Son of God, begotten of the Father, Only begotten, that is, from the substance of the Father; God from God, Light from Light, Very God from very God, begotten not made, Consubstantial ['homoousios'

6 The letter is quoted in J Stevenson (ed), *A New Eusebius: Documents Illustrative of the History of the Church to A.D. 337*, SPCK, 1960, p 345. Furthermore, the Council of Nicaea denounced anyone who claimed that (1) the Son was not eternal but there was a time when he did not exist, (2) the Son is a different essence than the Father, and (3) the Son was created and thus was not unchangeable like God. In fact, the early church condemned such beliefs and those who held them as heretical thus bound for hell.

= same essence] with the Father, by whom all things were made, both things in heaven and things in earth; who for us men and for our salvation came down and was incarnate, was made man, suffered, and rose again the third day, ascended into heaven, and is coming to judge the living and the dead.

And in the Holy Ghost.

It was now officially heresy to believe that the Son was created, or that he was not co-eternal with the Father. However, there was still ambiguity surrounding the definitions of some key terms—for example, "from the substance of the Father" remained ambiguous, as did the limited articulation of the third person of the Trinity, the Holy Spirit. The creed left some important theological questions unaddressed. What's more, the question remained: would the unity agreed upon by the council, at the instigation of the emperor, hold?

The storm after the calm: Arianism resurges after Nicaea

The theological ambiguity in the Nicene Creed of 325 AD opened the way for a controversy that would bubble on for nearly sixty years. It would take until the Council of Constantinople in 381 AD for the matter to finally be settled.

Because of the pressure exerted by Constantine, the unity created at Nicaea was paper-thin and fell apart soon after the council. In the attempt to gain unity, it was in fact lost, because there was no inherent agreement on the *words* and therefore *theological ideas* used in the creed. In many ways, this is one of the main ideas of this book. If there isn't agreement on the meaning of the words and their theological weight, there can only ever be a paper-thin, anaemic unity.

Soon after the council, Arianism resurfaced. Athanasius, who became bishop of Alexandria in 328 AD, led the way in trying to maintain the anti-Arian theology. For his troubles, he faced multiple exiles and was derided falsely.[7] Though Arius died in 336 AD, his teachings lived on in his followers, who further developed them.[8] By 357 AD, Arianism was the presiding teaching in the empire, and the Council of Sirmium held at the imperial residence that year forbade the use of the terms *homoousios* and *homoiousios*.

The church of the Roman Empire now appeared to be thoroughly Arian, though Athanasius' death in 373 AD likewise did not spell the end of the anti-Arian debate, which continued and was furthered in particular by three theologians born shortly after the Council of Nicaea, known collectively as the Cappadocian Fathers (Basil of Caesarea, Basil's younger brother Gregory, who was later Bishop of Nyssa and known as Gregory of Nyssa, and Gregory of Nazianzus).

---

7   One of the most bizarre rumours levelled against Athanasius was that he killed a bishop, then chopped off his hand in order to perform black magic. This particular rumour was luckily easily refuted by presenting the apparently dead bishop—who was actually alive—with both hands firmly attached to the rest of him.

8   Arius reportedly died on a public toilet with a terrible case of bowel trouble, which was a story that delighted his opponents.

THE NICENE CREED

Clearer skies: the Council of Constantinople settles the debate

Theodosius I, the new Roman emperor in 379 AD, wanted the matter settled. In 381 AD, he called the Council of Constantinople, which affirmed Nicaea and clarified the more ambiguous areas in the original Nicene Creed. The Cappadocian Fathers played a key role at Constantinople: they articulated the doctrine of the Trinity in wonderfully clear and thoughtful ways and made an enormous contribution to the early church in this regard.

The result of the Council of Constantinople is officially termed (somewhat wordily) the 'Nicene-Constantinopolitan Creed'. Today it's more often referred to as simply the Nicene Creed, but what we recite together in our church assemblies and study in our theological communities is the version of the creed finally settled upon in 381 AD.

Below is the version of the creed that you are likely familiar with. The additions from the Council of Constantinople are in italics so you can see how the creed evolved between the two councils:

We believe in one God the Father almighty, maker *of heaven and earth,* of all things visible and invisible;

And in one Lord Jesus Christ, the only-begotten Son of God, begotten from the Father *before all ages,* light from light, true God from true God, begotten not made, of one substance with the

Father, through Whom all things came into existence, Who because of us men and because of our salvation came down *from the heavens*, and was incarnate *from the Holy Spirit and the Virgin Mary* and became man, and was crucified *for us under Pontius Pilate*, and suffered and *was buried*, and rose again on the third day *according to the Scriptures* and ascended into heaven, and *sits on the right hand of the Father*, and will come again *with glory* to judge the living and dead, *of Whose kingdom there will be no end*;

And in the Holy Spirit, *the Lord and life-giver, Who proceeds from the Father [and the Son], who with the Father and the Son is together worshipped and together glorified, who spoke through the prophets; in one holy Catholic and apostolic Church. We confess one baptism to the remission of sins; we look forward to the resurrection of the dead and the life in the world to come.* Amen.[9]

It is this creed that the church has confessed throughout the centuries, and which has helped tether it

---

9 Taken from J Stevenson (ed), WHC Frend (revised), *Creeds, Councils and Controversies: Documents illustrating the history of the Church AD 337–461*, SPCK, 1989, pp 114–15. For further information on the differences between the two creeds, and particularly the significance of what was added in and what was left out, see chapter 10 in JND Kelly, *Early Christian Creeds* (T&T Clark, 2006). At the Synod of Toledo in Spain in 589 AD, the double procession of the Holy Spirit was clearly articulated, and the Nicene-Constantinopolitan Creed was amended to say that the Holy Spirit "proceeds from the Father and the Son".

theologically to the true nature of the Father, Son and Spirit in the Trinity.

What follows throughout this book is a closer examination of each of the theological statements in this creed so we can understand what each mean and what is at stake when the very words used are contested in terms of their theological meaning.

Questions for reflection or discussion

1. As you read through the Nicene-Constantinopolitan Creed, what strikes you most? In what ways can you see the creed refuting Arianism?

2. Reflect on John 1:1–18. How is God the Son depicted in this passage?

3. The Nicene Creed also helps us confess the divinity of the Holy Spirit. Read Acts 5:3–4. How do we see the divinity of God, the Holy Spirit, on display here? Can you think of other places in the Bible that attest to his divinity?

4. How does knowing God as three persons but one essence help you in your own daily Christian journey?

2

THE NICENE CREED UNDER THE AUTHORITY OF SCRIPTURE

Alastair Dunlop

Foundations matter. Just ask the person who wants to build a 2,240 square foot Georgian house, only to discover that foundations have been laid instead for a sprawling 5,450 square foot French château—this would be more than a small setback!

What we build is determined by the foundation. Reconfigure the foundation, and we reconfigure the entire shape and structure of the building. And of course, if the building is going to stand the test of time, the foundation must be right. So it is when it comes to our faith and practice as Christian people. This too has a foundation.

When we confess our faith in the Nicene Creed, we are taking a stand for what we believe to be the truth about God. But before we join together in saying what we stand *for*, we must be clear about what we stand *on*.

If we get the foundation of our faith and practice right, the church can fulfil its identity as "the pillar and foundation of the truth" (1 Tim 3:15). If we get the foundation wrong, we will sadly imitate the churches of Galatia, to whom Paul said, "I am astonished that you are so quickly deserting the one who called you to live in the grace of Christ and are turning to a different gospel" (Gal 1:6).

The only true foundation

In two of Paul's letters, he writes plainly about the foundation of the church:

> [God's] household [is] built on the foundation of the apostles and prophets,[1] with Christ Jesus himself as the chief cornerstone. (Eph 2:19b–20)

> For no-one can lay any foundation other than the one already laid, which is Jesus Christ. (1 Cor 3:11)

At a quick glance it may seem as if Paul is confused— is the foundation "the apostles and prophets", or is it

---

1 'Prophets' here are most likely New Testament prophets—see Ephesians 3:4b–5: "… the mystery of Christ … was not made known to the sons of men in other generations as it has now been revealed to his holy apostles and prophets by the Spirit". This would mean that New Testament prophets shared the foundational role given to the apostles—men like the prophet Silas (Acts 15:32; 1 Thess 1:1; 1 Pet 5:12). Consider also Luke and John Mark who were "inspired authors of Scripture who were not apostolic eye-witnesses and ear-witnesses of the Lord, but who, by the Spirit, laid down the foundational and final teaching of Christ for his church" (E Clowney, *The Church*, IVP, 1995, p 262).

"Jesus Christ"? But Paul isn't confused. The two statements shed light on each other, as Calvin explains:

> In the strict sense of the term, Christ is the only foundation ... He alone is the rule and standard of faith. But Christ is actually the foundation on which the church is built by the preaching of doctrine.[2]

It is the apostles' "preaching of doctrine"—their teaching about the person and work of Christ—that is the sole foundation of the church. For how could we know Christ Jesus if no-one had proclaimed him?

The apostles and prophets were sent by Christ, to preach Christ, with the authority of Christ (John 13:20; 2 Cor 5:19–20), having received the special revelation of Christ, by the Spirit of Christ (John 14:26; 16:13; Eph 3:5). Were it not for the apostolic preaching of Christ, there would be no true knowledge of Christ, and therefore no foundation on which to build the church.

As we see in the New Testament, the apostles preached the fullness of Christ Jesus: his humanity and deity, his mission and accomplishments, his miracles and teaching, his goodness and grace, his justice and rule, his death and resurrection, his ascension and intercession, his future return and heavenly kingdom. It's not hard to see that the content, theme, focus and delight of all their preaching was Christ!

---

2   J Calvin, 'Commentaries on the Epistle of Paul to the Ephesians and Galatians', Ephesians 2:20, trans. W Pringle, Christian Classics Ethereal Library (ccel.org/ccel/calvin/calcom41/calcom41.iv.iii.vi.html).

We preach Christ crucified. (1 Cor 1:23)

What we preach is not ourselves, but Jesus Christ as Lord. (2 Cor 4:5)

We are therefore Christ's ambassadors. (2 Cor 5:20)

It is this apostolic preaching of Christ that precedes and creates the church. It is her only true foundation.

This foundation is complete

This preaching of Christ through his apostles and prophets is a foundation that is "once for all entrusted to God's holy people" (Jude 1:3). There is nothing provisional or partial about this body of doctrine that Jude calls "the faith" (1:3). Given that Christ is the climax of God's special revelation (Heb 1:1–4), it cannot be enhanced or further progressed. Christ is God's full and final Word. No new apostles and prophets are needed, for there is no more foundation to be laid. This truth is beautifully captured by modern hymn-writers CityAlight:

What gift of grace is Jesus my redeemer,
There is no more for heaven now to give.[3]

That's exactly right. Having been delivered "once for all", this revelation is final and complete. And with it, we are blessed beyond measure. In Christ we have "every spiritual blessing" (Eph 1:3) and have "everything we need" for life and godliness (2 Pet 1:3). The church needs nothing else to rest and rely on.

3 CityAlight, 'Yet Not I but Through Christ in Me' [song], *Yet Not I and Other Songs for the Church*, 2018.

But there's an implicit warning here too. If the church adds to this "once for all" foundation of apostolic doctrine, it is moving beyond—and therefore departing from—God's final and complete revelation of himself in Jesus Christ.

This foundation is written

So how do we access this final and complete revelation of Jesus Christ, once for all delivered to the saints? We don't have a time-machine. We can't go back to hear the Lord Jesus and his apostles and prophets, nor can we bring them to us.

This is why God has caused his revelation to be preserved, passed on and proclaimed to us in the written words of the Bible. As Sinclair Ferguson puts it, without Scripture humankind "would forget, distort, and even destroy God's revelation of himself in space and history".[4] It is therefore inconceivable that God, in his kindness, would not give us his holy Scriptures.

Moreover, the Scriptures of the Old Testament are incomplete without the New Testament. Since Christ is the promise and theme of the Old Testament, and the crowning glory of God's revelation, how could his coming be then omitted from the Bible?

The Holy Spirit has given a complete Bible to the church to preserve God's spoken word. Having revealed the mystery of Christ to his apostles and prophets, and

4   S Ferguson, *Some Pastors and Teachers*, The Banner of Truth Trust, 2017, p 371.

having empowered and equipped them to proclaim it, the Spirit also enabled them to write it down exactly as he wanted (2 Pet 1:20-21). As Ferguson writes, "Apostleship existed in order to give Scripture to the church."[5]

Therefore, it is no surprise that Paul expected his letters to be read in church alongside the sacred writings of the Old Testament (Col 4:16), or that Peter referred to Paul's writings as Scripture (2 Pet 3:16). The New Testament writings self-consciously carry the same divine authority as the Old Testament. And what a gift of grace we have in the completed canon of Scripture (i.e. the complete collection of books that belong in the Bible)—for in the written word of God we meet the incarnate word of God, Jesus himself.

This brings us to the very heart of Reformation theology. Two of the rally cries of the Reformation were 'Scripture alone' and 'Christ alone'. Each one is bound up with the other. If our faith is not founded on Scripture alone, we will be led away from faith in Christ alone. When our faith is in Christ alone, it is according to Scripture alone. There is no way to pull apart these inseparable twins, 'Christ alone' and 'Scripture alone'. These are our one true foundation, our solid rock.

This foundation is supremely authoritative

The written word of God is not only the rock under our feet—it is also the supreme authority over our lives. In 2 Timothy Paul writes that "all Scripture is God-

---

5 Ferguson, *Some Pastors and Teachers*, p 356.

breathed" (3:16). This means that all Scripture is entirely the product of God's breath (Spirit), exhaled from the mouth of God, so to speak. All the words of Scripture are therefore "the very words of God" (Rom 3:2).

The doctrine of inspiration is not that God took some human writings and breathed *into* them, but rather that God breathed *out* the Scriptures through the agency of human authors. This does not mean that the human authors were mere secretaries to whom God dictated each sentence. On the contrary, they laboured with their own creativity and careful choice of words, applying their own hearts and minds in the service of God. But what they wrote was entirely of God. What Scripture says, God says. And since God is "the God of truth" (Isa 65:16, ESV), his word is infallible—it cannot err. This is why we can have absolute confidence that the Bible is entirely trustworthy and true—a quality that sets Scripture apart from every other authority.

Other authorities exist, of course, but none are infallible and flawless like the Bible. This was the underlying issue in all the disputes of the Protestant Reformation. "Has the pope not erred many times?" wrote Martin Luther in his tract to the Christian Nobility in 1520. He went on: "When the pope acts contrary to the Scriptures, it is our duty to stand by the Scriptures, to reprove him and to constrain him, according to the word of Christ, Matthew 18[:15–17]."[6]

6 M Luther, 'To the Christian Nobility of the German Nation Concerning the Reform of the Christian Estate', in Denis R Janz (ed), *A Reformation Reader: Primary Texts with Introductions*, second edn, Fortress Press, 2008, pp 100–101.

Similarly, John Calvin wrote to Emperor Charles V in 1544, saying, "We assert that those who preside over churches today under the name of bishops are not faithful guardians and ministers of godly doctrine, so much that instead, they are its fiercest enemies".[7]

To guard against false prophets and false teaching, the authorities of the church must be subordinated to the supreme authority of the Bible. Since only the Bible is the infallible, flawless word of God, there is no higher court of appeal. Therefore, the Bible must reign supreme over popes and councils in all matters of faith and practice.

But the Roman Catholic Church stands in opposition to this view. Its foundation and authority are not constituted by Scripture alone, but rather a three-legged stool of Scripture, tradition and the magisterium (the teaching office of Rome, consisting of the pope, bishops and councils). Tradition, according to Rome, is the teaching that is passed on orally from Christ and his apostles to the succession of bishops. While Scripture is the written part of this tradition, the other part is Rome's official teaching—the living voice of God's revelation that is defined by the magisterium, which both precedes and exceeds Scripture.

In this view, the Bible is not enough for knowledge of God and his ways. It is rather one part of a much larger whole. The faithful must look for divine revelation beyond the Bible—believing and obeying whatever

7 J Calvin, *The Necessity of Reforming the Church*, Reformation Trust Publishing, 2020, pp 49–50.

the Church teaches as the word of God. Look at how the Catechism of the Catholic Church explains it:

> The Church, to whom the transmission and interpretation of Revelation is entrusted, does not derive her certainty about all revealed truths from the holy Scriptures alone. Both Scripture and Tradition must be accepted and honoured with equal sentiments of devotion and reverence. (CCC 82)[8]

This view relegates the Bible from a place of supreme authority *over* the Church, to a place of relative importance *alongside* the Church. In effect, the Bible is relegated lower still, for although it is said to be equal with tradition, it is subsumed under the larger, living voice of the Church by which it is defined. As the catechism states:

> The task of giving an authentic interpretation of the Word of God, whether in its written form or in the form of Tradition, has been entrusted to the living, teaching office of the Church alone. Its authority in this matter is exercised in the name of Jesus Christ. (CCC 85)

Scripture, therefore, never has the final word. For example, the Roman Catholic doctrine of the immaculate

---

8 The Catechism of the Catholic Church (CCC) is a key reference work that summarizes the Catholic Church's teaching. This book uses the standard abbreviation 'CCC' for references to the catechism, followed by the number of the paragraph being referred to. References are taken from the version of the catechism published on the website of the Holy See, the central governing body of the Catholic Church. It can be accessed here: www.vatican.va/archive/ENG0015/_INDEX.HTM

conception, which states that Mary was without original sin, is not only without scriptural warrant but is also contrary to the clear teaching of Scripture (for more on this see chapter 7). Yet this teaching is binding on all Catholics, because in practice, tradition rules over Scripture.

The relationship of the Bible to the Church is therefore precisely the opposite of what it should be. It's upside-down. The Bible is not even necessary for the guidance and survival of the Church, for there is always the living tradition to bring heavenly light and direction.

Tragically, this has the result of immunizing the Church against biblical reform. How can true reform take place, when all must look to the Church, listen to the Church, submit to the Church? While Rome gladly affirms the divine authority of the Bible, it is actually the Church's voice that is pre-eminent and decisive, not the voice of Scripture.

The Roman Catholic Church therefore departs from the one true foundation of Scripture alone, which is not only infallible, flawless, supreme and final, but is also sufficient and clear, "able to make [us] wise for salvation through faith in Christ Jesus ... and is useful for teaching, rebuking, correcting and training in righteousness, so that the servant of God may be thoroughly equipped for every good work" (2 Tim 3:15–17).

Article 7 of the Belgic Confession (written in 1561) speaks on the issue with wonderful clarity:

> We believe that this Holy Scripture fully contains
> the will of God and that all that man must believe

in order to be saved is sufficiently taught therein. The whole manner of worship which God requires of us is written in it at length. It is therefore unlawful for any one, even for an apostle, to teach otherwise than we are now taught in Holy Scripture: yes, even if it be an angel from heaven, as the apostle Paul says (Gal 1:8). Since it is forbidden to add to or take away anything from the Word of God (Dt 12:32), it is evident that the doctrine thereof is most perfect and complete in all respects. We may not consider any writings of men, however holy these men may have been, of equal value with the divine Scriptures; nor ought we to consider custom, or the great multitude, or antiquity, or succession of times and persons, or councils, decrees or statutes, as of equal value with the truth of God, since the truth is above all ...[9]

This foundation is crucial for the creeds

First, let it be said that creeds are crucial in themselves. A creedless church is a clueless church. It is not that special revelation is lacking and needs to be enlarged in any way—it is simply that God's full and final word should be taught, defended and confessed.

But the creeds and confessions of the church must never be confused with its foundation. The Nicene Creed is so wonderful and worthy of confessing

9 Article 7 of the Belgic Confession, taken from the version found on the Westminster Seminary California website (wscal.edu/belgic-confession/).

precisely because its foundation is the Bible. The members of the Councils of Nicaea (325) and Constantinople (381) exercised a God-given authority and responsibility to teach only what is true to Scripture, and to oppose that which deviates from Scripture. The creed resulting from Nicaea is a precious gift to help us guard and teach what the Bible reveals about God. For 1700 years the creed has stood the test of time, as successive generations have recognized its fidelity to the Bible.

And yet even as we use the creed, we must still take care to believe it in a truly biblical way. For just as the words of Scripture can be twisted and distorted, so too can the words of the creed. The creed itself must be understood by the truth of holy Scripture, upon which it is founded.

Gresham Machen helps us to see the crucial distinction between Scripture and creeds:

> If we could imagine all the creeds of Christendom as having been suddenly wiped out of men's memories, so that we should have to start all over again in our understanding of the Bible and in our summary setting forth of what the Bible teaches, I believe that in time the necessary creeds of the church would again be built up. It might take another nineteen centuries—if it be God's will that the present age shall remain that long; it might take twice that time. But sooner or later it would be done. The Bible is the really essential thing; it is the foundation. The creeds of the church are the superstructure. Take away the

foundation, and all is lost. But take away the superstructure, and the superstructure can be built up again if the foundation remains.[10]

This foundation is essential for unity

The foundation *upon* which we stand, and the people *with* whom we stand, are inextricably connected. If we are standing on different foundations, are we really standing together? Do we even mean the same things when we use the same words? If we aim to have a shared understanding of words like 'salvation', we must begin by submitting to the same final authority.

The unity Jesus prays for in John 17:20–21 is the unity of those who will believe in the apostolic message. Similarly, when Paul refers to the apostolic foundation of the church in Ephesians 2:20, he emphasizes the profound unity that is built on that foundation. Who would have thought that Jews and Gentiles—people who were deeply alienated from each other—could become *one* in Jesus Christ? And yet that is what happens when fellowship is built on the foundation of the New Testament apostles and prophets. True unity is founded on the true gospel.

But if we will not stand together on Scripture alone, we'll have neither the gospel, nor unity. "We are thus enabled to distinguish between a true and a false church", says Calvin in his commentary on Ephesians

10 First published in *The Presbyterian Guardian*, vol 7, no 1, 10 January 1940; see also *Things Unseen*, Westminster Seminary Press, 2020, p 332.

2:20. "This is of the greatest importance; for the tendency to error is always strong, and the consequences of mistake are dangerous in the extreme."[11]

Calvin understood that a false foundation gives rise to a false gospel. And a false gospel gives rise to a false church. Foundations matter. May God unite his people in the truth of the gospel, as we stand together in Christ alone, on the foundation of Scripture alone.

Questions for reflection or discussion

1. Read Ephesians 2:19–20 and 1 Corinthians 3:10–15. What is the only true foundation of the church and why does it matter?

2. Read 2 Timothy 3:14–17 and 2 Peter 1:12–20. How can we trust the Bible, and only the Bible, to be entirely trustworthy and true?

3. What is the relationship of the Church to the Bible in Roman Catholicism? In what way is it upside-down? What does this mean for reform in the Roman Catholic Church?

4. Why is the 'Scripture alone' principle so important for Christian unity?

11 Calvin, 'Commentaries on the Epistle of Paul to the Ephesians and Galatians' (ccel.org/ccel/calvin/calcom41/calcom41.iv.iii.vi.html).

3

THE TRINITARIAN
FRAMEWORK OF
THE NICENE CREED

Leonardo De Chirico

We believe in one God,
the Father almighty,
maker of heaven and earth,
of all things visible and invisible.

And in one Lord Jesus Christ,
the only Son of God,
begotten from the Father before all ages.

...

And we believe in the Holy Spirit,
the Lord, the giver of life.
He proceeds from the Father and the Son,

and with the Father and the Son is worshiped and glorified.[1]

The Nicene Creed is built on the confession of God as one in nature and three in persons: Father, Son and Holy Spirit. Motivated to clarify the identity of Jesus Christ as the Son of God incarnate, the Council of Nicaea framed its recognition of Jesus Christ as having the same nature as the Father in the context of God as Trinity.

The profession of this trinitarian account of God has architectural significance for the Christian faith. All aspects of the Christian life (doctrine, ethics, liturgy, mission, church, worldview) are shaped by it. The Father's relationship to his Son and his Spirit stands behind everything about his relationship to us and the world, eternity and history, salvation and judgement. The biblical gospel stands or falls on the reality of God—creator, provider and redeemer—being the only and true God as Father, Son and Spirit.

Unlike the fourth-century heresy of Arianism, which depicted God as one and the Son as 'similar' but not equal to the Father in his deity, the Nicene Council understood biblical revelation as presenting God as both one and three. This articulation set a foundational parameter for Christian orthodoxy for the church to

---

1   In this book we quote from the version of the Nicene Creed found on the Christian Reformed Church website (crcna.org/welcome/beliefs/creeds/nicene-creed). This version of the creed is very similar in word choice to the one found in Norman Tanner (ed.), *Decrees of the Ecumenical Councils* (vol 1, Sheed & Ward, 1990, p 24), which is part of a Roman Catholic standard collection of church documents.

build on in subsequent centuries.[2]

Today, the trinitarian confession of the Christian faith is often assumed to belong to all mainstream forms of Christianity—Roman Catholic, Orthodox and Protestant. In one sense, this is true. Formally speaking, all Christian bodies (be they single congregations, denominations or councils/federations of churches) representing Christianity for the past 1,000 years have adhered to the trinitarian core of the Nicene Creed. They have embedded it in their confessional standards, recite it, and use it in their teaching and liturgies.

Protestant and Catholic Christianity

In his survey of the Protestant tradition, Scott Swain argues that the Reformers ...

> ... were committed to the doctrine [of the Trinity]'s traditional modes of expression and to its propagation in the Protestant church. Many of the major Protestant confessions produced in the sixteenth century employed tradition and affirmed the early creeds as reliable summaries of biblical teaching.[3]

In other words, we can say that Protestant Christianity is Nicene Christianity because it is rooted in the trinitarian foundations of the biblical faith.

2 For more on this, see L Ayres, *Nicaea and its Legacy: An Approach to Fourth-Century Trinitarian Theology*, Oxford University Press, 2004.
3 S Swain, 'The Reformers and the Ecumenical Doctrine of the Trinity', in G Emery and M Levering (eds), *The Oxford Handbook of the Trinity*, Oxford University Press, 2011, p 228.

What about Roman Catholicism? In their widely acclaimed book *Is the Reformation Over?*, Mark Noll and Carolyn Nystrom survey the contents of the 1992 Catechism of the Catholic Church (CCC), an important reference work that summarizes the teaching of the Catholic Church. Noll and Nystrom argue that evangelicals can embrace at least two-thirds of this catechism.[4]

This alleged consensus stems from a 'common orthodoxy' based on the ancient trinitarian creeds, like Nicaea, which articulate the triune nature of God, the incarnation of Jesus Christ as the God-man, the need for salvation, the reality of the church, the hope of eternal salvation, and so on. This is to say that Roman Catholicism allegedly espouses Nicene—and therefore trinitarian—Christianity. Indeed, the first part of the Catechism of the Catholic Church is a commentary on the creed and is structured under these headings:

- "I believe in God the Father" (section 2, chapter 1). This chapter includes articles on God the Father, God the Almighty, heaven and earth, as well as man and the Fall.
- "I believe in Jesus Christ, the Only Son of God" (section 2, chapter 2). This chapter includes articles on the incarnation, the virgin Mary, and the life, crucifixion, burial, descent into hell, resurrection and ascension of Jesus Christ, as well as the last judgement.

---

4 M Noll and C Nystrom, *Is the Reformation Over? An Evangelical Assessment of Roman Catholicism*, Baker Academic, 2005, p 119. For an additional evangelical assessment of the catechism, see G Allison, *Roman Catholic Theology and Practice: An Evangelical Assessment*, Crossway, 2014.

- "I believe in the Holy Spirit" (section 2, chapter 3). This chapter includes articles on the Holy Catholic Church, the communion of the saints, Mary, the forgiveness of sin, the resurrection of the body and eternal life.

This first part of the catechism is structured according to the wording of the Nicene Creed, and this pattern seemingly permeates the rest of the catechism. But before we rush to the conclusion that evangelicals and Catholics embrace the same trinitarian faith on this basis, let's look more closely at the Catholic Catechism's trinitarian confession, as well as what comes before and after it.

1. What *precedes* the trinitarian confession is misconceived

Before it refers to the Trinity, chapter 1 of the catechism opens with a programmatic statement that man is *capax Dei*, or 'capable of God'—that is, man is naturally oriented towards God. This is not only the recognition of the religious dimension of human life but the belief in the inherent openness of humanity to God. Indeed, in their natural capacity for God, human beings are thought of as having an innate and permanent desire for God.

Certainly, Roman Catholic theology recognizes the debilitating effects of sin, but sin is not so bad that it undermines the ability of every man and woman to be 'capable' of God. Because of sin's limited impact, grace finds in our nature a receptive attitude. Although sin has touched nature, the latter is still programmatically open to be infused, elevated and supplemented by God's grace. This 'nature-grace interdependence', in all its various forms and degrees, is the reason why Roman Catholicism is optimistic about a human being's ability to know God, to follow his will, and to cooperate with his grace. Roman Catholicism has a strong view of the intrinsic openness of nature, but a mild view of sin (see CCC 1849–1875).[5]

Because nature is seen as 'open' to grace, it follows that the physical world can be seen to transmit the grace of God. It is because of this that even an inanimate object like bread can be seen to become the body of Christ during the Eucharist. This openness of nature to grace also helps explain the ability of Roman Catholicism to embrace and integrate the whole of humanity into its liturgies, practices and devotions (meaning that the Catholic Church often falls into syncretism as result).[6]

Rome holds a view of nature that is tainted by sin but not depraved, obscured but not blinded, wounded but not alienated, morally disordered but not spiritually dead, inclined to evil but still having a 'capacity' for God. By changing our understanding of how we relate to God, we are most fundamentally changing our understanding *of God*: who is this trinitarian God, and how does he therefore relate to us?

5 All references to the Catechism of the Catholic Church (CCC) can be found at www.vatican.va/archive/ENG0015/_INDEX.HTM. The number following 'CCC' refers to the paragraph being quoted.
6 On the 'nature-grace interdependence', see Allison, *Roman Catholic Theology and Practice*, pp 46–55.

It is no coincidence that the Roman Catholic understanding of salvation has always prioritized 'participatory' categories that presuppose our cooperation with grace. It has always refused the 'declarative' categories that focus on the primacy of grace alone and the imputation of Christ's righteousness on the sinner.

This is, of course, in contrast to the evangelical emphasis which sees that, while we retain our *imago Dei*, we have radically and permanently lost our natural capacity for God unless God himself regenerates it in our hearts. We find ourselves under God's righteous judgement without any ability to bypass it ourselves.

Rather than the *capax Dei*, the evangelical faith insists on the *coram Deo* ('in the presence of God') dimension of life. Our life is before God, whose presence cannot be avoided whenever we try to escape him. We are always inexcusable. It is Christ's righteousness, external to us, that saves us. This gift must be received by faith alone.

Here is the first crossroad that radically separates the Catholic and evangelical perspectives. Before we even get to any explicit reference to the Trinity in Catholic thought, we see that this prior commitment of Roman Catholicism shapes all that follows in terms of its doctrine and practice.

2. What is *contained* in the trinitarian confession is puzzling

Christ and the Holy Spirit

So what happens when we do get to an explicit trinitarian confession in the Catechism of the Catholic Church?

We've already touched on what is covered in the catechism under each heading of Father, Son and Holy Spirit. Looking more closely under each heading, we see that in the chapter on Jesus Christ, the Roman Catholic teaching on Mary is presented in terms of her *own* immaculate conception (CCC 490–493) and her perpetual virginity (CCC 496–507). In the subsequent chapter on the Holy Spirit, we find that Mary is the "Mother of the Church" who was bodily assumed[7] and is to be venerated (CCC 963–972) to the point of arguing that "the Church's devotion to the Blessed Virgin is intrinsic to Christian worship" (CCC 971). What does the insertion of this Catholic Mariology—the study of Mary—in the articles on Christ and the Holy Spirit mean? It shows that for Rome, Mariology is inseparable from trinitarian doctrine. In a sense, the Catholic confession of Christ and the Holy Spirit opens the way for the Roman Catholic elevation of Mary. Mariology is not a separate attachment to the trinitarian foundation but an organic part of the Roman Catholic account of it. For evangelicals, much of Roman Catholic Mariology is an unwarranted development away from Scripture and, therefore, in contrast with the biblical revelation of God as one and three.

Despite the intention not to divert attention from the Son and the Spirit, Mariology tends to be an intruder into trinitarian harmony and an obstacle to

---

7   The assumption of Mary is the belief that because she was without the stain of original sin, Mary's body and soul were assumed up into heaven at the end of her earthly life, and she didn't suffer the corruption of the grave as a consequence of sin. (For more on the virgin Mary, see chapter 7.)

fully appreciating who the triune God is and what he has done for us. Jesus says, "Come to me" (Matt 11:28) and "no-one comes to the Father except through me" (John 14:6), but Roman Catholicism encourages people to invoke Mary for help. The Holy Spirit intercedes for us (Rom 8:26–27), but Mary is approached as an intercessor.[8]

Evangelicals and Catholics may recite the same trinitarian formulations of the Nicene Creed, but there are fundamental differences in how they appreciate its significance, not least because major components of Roman Catholic Mariology are found in the Catholic view of the Trinity.

The church

The other important offshoot of the Roman Catholic understanding of the Trinity is its doctrine of the church. In the Catholic Catechism, the blueprint of Rome's view of church stems from the chapter on the Holy Spirit (CCC 748–959). Roman Catholic ecclesiology (the study of the church) is embedded in the Roman Catholic doctrine of the Spirit not only in its general contours (e.g. the church as the people of God, the body of Christ and the temple of Holy Spirit) but also in the specific Roman features (e.g. its hierarchical nature and the papacy).

---

8 More on how Roman Catholic Mariology undermines the trinitarian account of God can be found in my book *A Christian's Pocket Guide to Mary: Mother of God?*, Christian Focus, 2017, pp 83–87.

If Jesus Christ is truly man and truly God (as affirmed in the creed), the catechism argues that the Roman Catholic Church, by virtue of "no weak analogy", is also "one complex reality which coalesces from a divine and a human element".[9] In the words of a papal document of Pius XII from 1943, the Church subsists almost like "another Christ".[10] Thus, the Catholic Church's understanding of itself is based on a Christological point. As Jesus Christ is fully man and fully God, so the Church is a *theandric* (human and divine) organism united to Christ and one with him.

The emphasis on this 'Christ-Church interconnection' seems to forget that the church is still a divine *creature*, belonging to the reality created by God and marked by sin, while Christ is the divine *Creator*, the one from whom all things are created, and who is perfect now and always.[11]

It's key that we appreciate the distinction between Creator and creature in order to avoid falling into the trap of elevating the church into a quasi-divine body. As French theologian Henri Blocher argues, in Roman Catholicism, a "larval monophysitism" manifests itself

9   *Lumen gentium* 8. (*Lumen gentium*, 'The Dogmatic Constitution on the Church', is one of the principal documents of the Second Vatican Council from 1964. It can be accessed on the website of the Holy See: www.vatican.va/archive/hist_councils/ii_vatican_council/documents/vat-ii_const_19641121_lumen-gentium_en.html)

10 '*Mystici Corporis Christi*: Encyclical of Pope Pius XII on the Mystical Body of Christ', para 53 (www.vatican.va/content/pius-xii/en/encyclicals/documents/hf_p-xii_enc_29061943_mystici-corporis-christi.html).

11 On the 'Christ-Church interconnection', see Allison, *Roman Catholic Theology and Practice*, pp 56–66.

—that is, the church is attributed divine traits that override human ones.[12] Thus we see that while Rome may confess the historical Jesus Christ as the Son of God become man and the Holy Spirit as God, the Catholic Church uses the same 'Christ' and the same 'Spirit' to support other doctrines and practices that are not biblical.[13]

Noll and Nystrom admit that when the catechism speaks of Christ, it interweaves him with the Church to the point of making them one.[14] This intermingling is unacceptable for evangelicals, who consider the exaltation of a created reality to be idolatry. On this extension of the meaning of 'Christ' in the catechism, Rome believes that the Church is endowed with the authority of Christ the King, the priesthood of Christ the Mediator, and the truth of Christ the Prophet. The catechism gives voice only to *this* interpretation of the Nicene faith.

While on first inspection we might observe an apparent 'common orthodoxy' based on the Catholic Church's trinitarian confession of faith, we don't have to look far to see that actually there is a profound difference in how we view the doctrines of Christ and the Holy Spirit (and therefore the Trinity).

---

12 H Blocher, *La doctrine de l'Église e des sacrements*, vol 1, Edifac, 2023, p 151. 'Monophysitism' was the heresy according to which the divine nature of Christ had swallowed the human nature. Applied to the church, "larval monophysitism" means that the Roman Catholic view of the church is at risk of elevating the divine prerogatives of the church over its human elements. Blocher further argues that "Roman theology is too little Trinitarian" (p 156).

13 For more on this, see especially chapters 4 and 5 (on the person and work of Jesus Christ) and chapter 6 (on the Holy Spirit).

14 Noll and Nystrom, *Is the Reformation Over?*, pp 147–149.

3. What *follows* the trinitarian confession is flawed

After the deviating premise of our capacity for God, and after the compromising interpretation of the Trinity as the source for Catholic Mariology and ecclesiology, the rest of the catechism gives voice to the standard Roman Catholic teaching on the sacraments, life in Christ, the human community, salvation, the ten commandments and prayer. The evangelical faith has significantly different accounts of how the ordinances of baptism and the Lord's Supper work, how we are justified by faith alone, and how we are gathered in the church. The catechism uses arguments from the Trinity to support its contradictory theology on each of these points.[15] Thus we can see that Rome's account of the Trinity leads to doctrines and practices that are distant, if not opposed, to the evangelical faith.

Nicene Christianity as a common ground?

A common refrain in ecumenical discourse is that all historical religious traditions (Roman Catholicism, Eastern Orthodoxy, various branches of Protestantism) differ in the way they understand salvation (e.g. justification, renewal, deification), as well as the nature and role of the church and the sacraments, but they agree on the tenets of the Christian doctrines of the Trinity and Christology.

---

15 For example, see the catechism's sections on the sacramental economy (1077–1109), on grace and justification (1987–2011), on the magisterium of the Roman Catholic Church (2032–2040).

While this is true at one level, we've seen that a closer look shows some cracks in this widespread assumption. While it is true that the contrast between the various interpretations of the creed becomes more evident in the areas of salvation and the church, both are inextricably related to trinitarian doctrine as the core of Christian theology.

As Gerald Bray puts it, "The great issues of Reformation theology—justification by faith, election, assurance of salvation—can be properly understood only against the background of Trinitarian theology which gave these matters their peculiar importance".[16] Against this background, the alleged consensus on the trinitarian framework of the Christian faith is more limited than often thought.

All attempts to point to 'Nicene Christianity' and 'creedal orthodoxy' as the common ground between Roman Catholicism and evangelicalism are historically simplistic and theologically superficial. How the trinitarian framework is received, believed and applied indicates a significant distance between the two traditions despite formal points of agreement. The words used are the same, but the theological worlds they open are different.[17]

16 G Bray, *The Doctrine of God*, IVP, 1993, pp 197–198. On this crucial point see also M Reeves, "The Holy Trinity" in M Barrett (ed.), *Reformation Theology: A Systematic Summary*, Crossway, 2017, pp 189–216.
17 For more on this point, see my book *Same Words, Different Worlds: Do Roman Catholics and Evangelicals Believe the Same Gospel?*, IVP, 2021.

Questions for reflection or discussion

Read Ephesians 1:1–14.

1. Highlight the places where you find mention of the Father, the Son and the Holy Spirit.

2. What does each person of the Trinity do in this passage?

3. This letter is addressed to "the saints" (or Christians) in Ephesus (v 1, ESV). What is the role of the saints in this passage?

4. If we were able to choose God for ourselves, how might that undermine the work of each person of the Trinity that you listed in question 2?

4
THE PERSON OF
JESUS CHRIST

Matthew Johnston

We believe ... in one Lord, Jesus Christ,
the only Son of God,
begotten from the Father before all ages,
God from God,
Light from Light,
true God from true God,
begotten, not made;
of the same essence as the Father.
Through him all things were made.

"Well, at least we have the same Christ." I've often heard this sentiment—or some variation of it—expressed in conversations between Roman Catholics and evangelicals. I can recall the first time our dear friends invited us over for dinner. It was the first of many such occasions and it was also the first time they had shared their table with Protestants (there aren't many of us in Italy). Later they confessed that, before we came over, they had sought the permission of a priest who told them, "We have significant differences, but we share the most important thing: Christ".

This priest's encouragement was perfectly understandable. There are some doctrines wherein we share nothing or almost nothing (the papacy, purgatory and the assumption of Mary). Compared to these doctrines, it can certainly be said that we share more when it comes to Christology (the study of Christ's person and work). Indeed, this is why the Nicene Creed is so enticing as an ecumenical tool: it focuses on the person of Christ. However, although the Council of Nicaea does point to elements of a shared Christology, it also presses us to reflect on key differences in the way Christology has developed in the history of the Church among various theological traditions.

Do Roman Catholics and evangelicals have the same Christ?

Before taking on the Christology of the Nicene Creed, we need to answer a question that will prepare us to read the creed carefully: do we have the same Christ? There is a great Italian word that helps us with our response: 'ni'. It's a mix of 'sì' (yes) and 'no'. Yes *and* no. In this case, it isn't a flimsy non-answer or an evasive side-step. Rather, it underscores the complexity of the question and the need for nuance.

We can respond with 'yes' and 'no', but in distinct

ways. We might respond 'yes' because we have a shared historical heritage and therefore share broad, general Christological expressions. On the other hand, we might respond 'no' because of the divergent ways Christology has developed in the history of the Church. Different theological traditions understand the person of Christ in different ways.

Yes

The positive response to our question contains two elements, one historical and the other theological. Historically, both evangelicals and Roman Catholics accept the earliest creeds as an authority on Christology: the Apostles' Creed and the Athanasian Creed, together with the Nicene Creed. Don't forget that the Reformers were keen to call themselves 'catholic' (with a lowercase 'c') and quick to underscore their disdain for theological novelty.[1]

This shared creedal heritage can be seen in the various catechetical traditions—both the Heidelberg Catechism (1563) and the Catechism of the Council of Trent (1566) are based, in large part, on the Apostles' Creed.[2] Evangelicals follow the Reformers who accepted the Council of Nicaea in what it decreed about the

---

1   See for example the Augsburg Confession (1530) in Chad Van Dixhoorn, *Creeds, Confessions and Catechisms: A Reader's Edition*, Crossway, 2022, p 48. The Augsburg Confession affirms: "There is nothing that varies from the Scriptures, or from the Church Catholic". On the distinction between 'Roman' and 'catholic' see KJ Collins and JL Walls, *Roman but not Catholic: What is at Stake 500 Years after the Reformation*, Baker Academic, 2017.

2   This is also the case for the Catechism of the Catholic Church (1992).

incarnation of God's Son because they "found that nothing is defined or established there which is not taught by the divinely inspired Scriptures".[3]

Both evangelical and Roman Catholic traditions share Christological 'grammar'—that is, they both employ the same terminology in their speech about Christ. The divine Son is *consubstantial* with the Father—that is, he is truly God, just as the Father is truly God. Jesus is *begotten*, not made—that is, he is eternally generated by the Father.

Both traditions also share the same Christological 'guardrails' introduced at Nicaea and expanded on in subsequent councils (most importantly Chalcedon): Christ is one divine person, the second person of the Trinity, who has two natures—one divine, the other human. These truths are the guardrails that must guide our reflections on the person of Christ and will protect us from error. This base-level theological overlap is what enables evangelicals to benefit from the work of Catholic theologians in Christology.

No

The negative response to the question, 'Do we have the same Christ?' is likewise both historical and theological.

Firstly, this shared acceptance of the earliest expressions of Christology does not guarantee that all following doctrinal developments are also shared. Quite a lot

3 PM Vermigli, 'Letter No. 267: To Polish Noblemen', in JP Donnelly (ed and trans), *Peter Martyr Vermigli: Life, Letters, and Sermons*, Thomas Jefferson University Press, 1999, p 202.

of Christological reflection transpired between 325 and the beginning of the Reformation in 1517, to say nothing of the 1700 years that separate 2025 from Nicaea. Nor should it be assumed that post-Nicene Christological developments were always linear or that everyone saw things the same way.

For example, in the first several hundred years after Nicaea it was normal to say that Christ was sinlessly ignorant of some things, but by the beginning of the 7th century that belief was deemed heretical.[4] The Reformers returned to this earlier teaching at key points.

To confess the Christ of Nicaea is good insofar as it goes, but it is at best a first step. A thoughtful Roman Catholic would never confine himself to Nicaea's teaching on the Bishop of Rome to construct his doctrine of the papacy.[5] Likewise, neither would they confine themselves only to Nicaea's teaching when it comes to reflections on the person of Christ. We too should consider Nicaea only a starting point for understanding the person of Christ.

Secondly, shared acceptance of the basic building blocks of Christology does not require agreement on the specific and detailed expositions and applications of these starting points. The significance of what we share

4   See Gregory the Great's letter to Eulogius in *Epistles of St Gregory of the Great*, book X, letter 39, NewAdvent.org (newadvent.org/fathers/360210039.htm).
5   See especially Canon 6 of the Council of Nicaea, which does not seem to accord the Bishop of Rome privileges beyond other bishops (*Nicene and Post Nicene Fathers*, series 2, vol 14, Eerdmans, p 15); cf. E Duffy, *Saints and Sinners: A History of the Popes*, Yale University Press, 2006. Duffy notes that "The Pope had played no part at Nicaea" (p 30).

in general (the grammar and guardrails mentioned above) must be assessed in light of the specific ways these doctrines are expounded.[6] We agree that Christ is true God and true man, but do we agree on why he *had* to be so for our salvation?

The doctrine of the person of Christ is interwoven with other doctrines, such that we shouldn't be surprised to find differences in Christology in the midst of so many other differences. For example, fundamental disagreements on the nature of the body of Christ, the Church, cannot be compartmentalized because they have implications for our understanding of the head of the body.

The beauty of Nicene Christology

In 1544, not long after his transalpine journey to flee the Roman Inquisition, the Italian Reformer Peter Martyr Vermigli penned a pastoral exposition on the Apostles' Creed. He observed that the twelve articles of this creed were "spoken, read and heard every day" but that "for the most part, or only rarely are they really savored".[7]

The present-day use of the Nicene Creed is comparable. If we are to savour the Christ of the Nicene Creed, there must be appreciation and anticipation.

---

6   W Cunningham, *Historical Theology: A Review of the Principal Doctrinal Discussions in the Christian Church Since the Apostolic Age*, Banner of Truth Trust, 1994, vol 2, p 112. Cunningham helpfully makes this point in his appraisal of the Council of Trent's teaching on justification.

7   PM Vermigli, *Una Semplice Dichiarazione sopra gli XII Articoli della Fede Cristiana*, Johan Hervagius, 1544, p 5: "ogni dì si dicono, leggono, & odono, & pella maggior parte mai, ò di rado ben si gustano".

Appreciation because its creedal formulae give us windows onto the glory of the person of Christ. *Anticipation* because the creed itself, which was never intended to be the final word on Christology, should create an eagerness to know more.

Appreciation

The body of the creed fixes its gaze on one person, one singular subject: "one Lord Jesus Christ". He is the Lord (*Kyrios*) who revealed himself to Abraham, Moses and David. Jesus, the name given to him at his birth, makes known that he is the last Adam who will save those who walk in darkness because of the fall of the first Adam. He is the Christ, the bearer of all three anointed offices: Prophet, Priest and King.

The creed makes clear that this Lord Jesus Christ is the only *begotten* Son of God. Some evangelicals might not immediately recognize the 'only begotten' language which is taken from John's Gospel (1:14, 18; 3:16) because certain modern English translations render *monogenēs* ('only begotten') as simply 'only' (e.g. ESV, NIV). However, the Nicene Creed emphasizes the Son's 'begottenness', using this language two times: Jesus is "begotten from the Father before all ages" and "begotten, not made".[8]

Jesus is "of the same essence [or substance] as the Father". That is to say, what the Father is, so also is Jesus. The creed employs the Creator-creature distinction to

---

8 On the translation of *monogenes* see CL Irons, "A Lexical Defense of the Johannine 'Only Begotten'" in F Sanders and S Swain (eds), *Retrieving Eternal Generation*, Zondervan, 2017, pp 98–116.

safeguard his deity. He is outside of the creation, just as the Father is, because everything that is has come into being through him (John 1:3; Col 1:16).

Christ is God just as the Father is God. But he isn't the Father. He's *from* (*ek*) the Father: Light *from* (*ek*) Light and true God *from* (*ek*) true God. Don't miss the importance of the preposition 'from' here. The movement in these statements happens in a single direction. This highlights the unique relationship between God the Father and God the Son. The Son is the word of the Father, the image of the Father, and the radiance of the glory of the Father (John 1:1; Col 1:15; Heb 1:3). Yet, it cannot be said that the Father is the word, image or radiance of the Son, any more than it can be said that the Son sent the Father.

All this to say: the creed makes clear that the Son is God, but he is distinct from the Father. The theologians of the fourth century didn't yet have the theological vocabulary to describe these distinctions (it would be some time before 'person' would become a standardized term to speak about God's 'threeness'). Yet we see in the creed that the seeds are present for the development of a more nuanced Christological articulation over time.[9]

The creed then moves to show that the one who is eternally begotten of the Father leaves heaven to be 'enfleshed' by (*ek*) the Holy Spirit and the Virgin Mary. The Son does not cease to be that which he is. He becomes that which he was not: a true man. The creed

9 On the theological development of the language see: Letham, *The Holy Trinity*, P&R Publishing, 2004, pp 115–121.

THE NICENE CREED

rightly couches his incarnation in soteriological termi-nology: "for us and for our salvation". The incarnation is ultimately postlapsarian—that is, the truths it pro-claims are framed as a 'response' to the fall. The one who knew only the acclamations of angels became a man and experienced the humiliation of death by crucifixion.

The fact that the creed proclaims all these magnifi-cent truths about Christ should fill us with admiration.

Anticipation

There is, however, something a bit lopsided about the Christology we find in the creed. There are some key missing pieces in its articulation of the person and work of Christ. Yet perhaps it's unfair to have expect-ed any more from Nicaea. As Lewis Ayres notes, the Nicene Fathers did not set out to write the definitive expression of Christology: "The idea that the creed would serve as a universal and precise marker of Chris-tian faith was unlikely to have occurred to anyone at Nicaea simply because the idea that any creed might so serve was as yet unheard of".[10]

Ayres explains that the goals of the council were significantly more modest: Nicaea's creed "was not designed to do much more than: (a) earn the approval (however grudging) of a majority present and (b) make it clear that certain perceived errors of Arius and

10 L Ayres, *Nicaea and its Legacy: An Approach to Fourth-Century Trinitarian Theology*, Oxford University Press, 2004, p 85. Ayres goes on to explain that the creed's usage as such was still evolving at the end of the fourth century (p 86).

his early supporters were unacceptable".[11] The key perceived error was a denial of the deity of Christ, which explains the emphasis on his deity in the creed.

Nicaea is a "window onto the confusion and complexity of the early fourth-century theological debates and not a revelation that a definitive turning-point had been reached".[12] This is why to read Nicaea correctly is to be filled with anticipation. Nicaea is a key point on a journey that is just beginning—a sapling, not an oak tree. Although the next ecumenical council—Constantinople I in 381 AD—still focused on dealing with Arianism (which was still very prevalent in the Church) and confirming the teaching of Nicaea, the next two councils—Ephesus in 431 AD and Chalcedon in 451 AD—picked up where Nicaea left off and further developed aspects of its Christology. How are we to understand Christ's human nature and does it include a rational soul? How are we to understand the relationship between Christ's two natures? These were the questions that the Council of Chalcedon began to answer.[13]

The Council of Chalcedon confessed:

> ... our Lord Jesus Christ [to be] the same perfect in Godhead and also in manhood; truly God and truly man, of a reasonable soul and body ... to be acknowledged in two natures, *inconfusedly, unchangeably, indivisibly, inseparably*, the distinction

11 Ayres, *Nicaea and its Legacy*, p 99.
12 Ayres, *Nicaea and its Legacy*, p 93.
13 The Council of Chalcedon certainly did not provide all the answers. Constantinople III (in 681 AD) would have to answer the question of the number of Christ's wills.

of the two natures being by no means taken away by the union ...[14]

The Chalcedon Council taught that Jesus' human nature includes a reasonable or rational soul whose faculties—namely intellect and will—are not swallowed up by his divine nature. While a debate about Christ's psychology may seem impractical, it's important to recall that Chalcedon was responding to an array of heresies and, significantly, the truth that a soulless Christ can't save those whose sins are more than skin deep. As Gregory of Nazianzen has famously declared, "That which is not assumed is not healed".[15]

The Council of Nicaea is certainly to be admired, but with an anticipation of what was to follow because it paved the way for the development of a richer Christology. Even after the Council of Chalcedon, there was still much work to do.

The person of Christ according to the Reformers

Both the Reformers and their Roman Catholic counterparts unreservedly confessed the Chalcedon Creed but they appropriated different aspects of it in ways that were compatible with their broader theological systems.

Roman Catholic theologians tended to place the

14 The Chalcedonian Definition, quoted in Schaff, *The Creeds of Christendom: The Greek and Latin Creeds*, vol 2, Baker, 2007, p 62.
15 'To Cledonius the Priest Against Apollinarius' in *Select Letters of Saint Gregory of Nazianzen* in P Schaff (ed), *Nicene and Post-Nicene Fathers*, series 2, vol 7, p 440 (ccel.org/ccel/schaff/npnf207.iv.ii.iii.html).

emphasis on the *unity* of Christ's two natures and the uniqueness of Christ's humanity to such an extent that they were accused of blurring the lines between humanity and deity.

Reformed theologians tended to place the emphasis on the *distinction* of Christ's natures to such an extent that they were accused of undermining the hypostatic union (the heresy called 'Nestorianism').[16] However, Reformed theology's "sharp distinction" between Christ's two natures seems far more congruous with the Chalcedon Definition, and by extension, Nicaea.[17]

John Calvin (1509–1564), along with other Reformed theologians, retrieved an ancient teaching on Christ's soul, which allowed him to understand the full picture of the Christ depicted in the Gospel narratives. Calvin taught that Christ really was ignorant of some things (Matt 24:36) and that he really grew in knowledge (Luke 2:52). As we touched on briefly above, that belief was later deemed untenable, but it seems to be the same position held by Athanasius, that great defender of Nicene Christology: "It is proper to man to be ignorant, just as being hungry and other things".[18]

---

16 "Reformed theologians" are specified here (as opposed to Protestant theologians more broadly) because Lutheran Christology developed along different lines.

17 H Bavinck, *Reformed Dogmatics: Sin and Salvation in Christ* (J Bolt ed, J Vriend trans), vol 3, Baker Academic, 2006, p 259.

18 Athanasius, 'Epistle Two-Three' in CRB Shapland (trans), *The Letters of Saint Athanasius Concerning the Holy Spirit*, The Epworth Press, 1951, p 166 (ia601306.us.archive.org/0/items/TheLettersOfSaintAthanasius ConcerningTheHolySpirit/Athanasius_Letters_to_Serapion_Shapland. pdf).

Robert Bellarmine (1542–1621), who was probably the most important defender of post-Tridentine Roman Catholicism, wrote against Calvin's position.[19] For Bellarmine, Christ did not learn anything experientially that he did not already know in another way. Bellarmine argued that if Christ's humanity was really in personal union with his deity, then he must have known more than any other man before him, even from his conception.

Bellarmine liked Calvin's teaching on the suffering of Christ's soul even less. Calvin taught that Christ's soul had to be capable of feeling the severity of divine judgement:

> In short, since neither as God alone could he feel death, nor as man alone could he overcome it, he coupled human nature with divine that to atone for sin he might submit the weakness of the one to death; and that, wrestling with death by the power of the other nature, he might win victory for us.[20]

Bellarmine, in contrast to Calvin, prioritized Christ's bodily suffering and saw Christ as suffering only in a part of his soul. Christ couldn't suffer in his whole soul because its upper part had always experienced the

19 Bellarmine was so important that more than 200 Protestant authors felt the need to respond to his writings. For more on Bellarmine see L De Chirico, 'Robert Bellarmine and his Controversies with the Reformers: A Window on Post-Tridentine Roman Catholic Apologetics', *European Journal of Theology*, 2002, 31(1):21–42.

20 J Calvin, *Institutes of the Christian Religion*, 1.12.3, in JT McNeill (ed), John Knox Press, 2006 (reissued), p 466.

'beatific vision'—the joyous state of the saints in glory who behold God face-to-face. This idea might sound strange to modern ears, but it was a common tenet of medieval Christology. To cite one example, Peter Lombard (d. circa 1160) so emphasized Christ's possession of the beatific vision in his earthly ministry that he said Christ's post-resurrection soul was not more blessed in the contemplation of God than his pre-resurrection soul.[21] Although some post-Vatican II Roman Catholic theologians distanced themselves from the doctrine of the beatific vision in Christ's soul from conception, it is not without its significant modern defenders, even today.[22]

Francis Turretin (1623–1687) was a Reformed theologian who wrote in response to Robert Bellarmine. He argued that Roman Catholics maintained their position on Christ's beatific vision "more easily to deny that spiritual sufferings were felt by the soul of Christ".[23] For Turretin, it was key that Christ's suffering wasn't downplayed: confusion about the person of Christ creates confusion about how Christ accomplished redemption. Reformed evangelical Christology was developed in light of the doctrine of Christ's two states (*status duplex*)—humiliation and exaltation. The elements of this doctrine are present in the Nicene Creed: Christ came down from heaven, suffered, died and was buried in his humiliation; he was raised, ascended to heaven

---

21 Lombard, *Sententiarum libri quattuor*, III.XVII.2–3.
22 For example, see SF Gaine, *Did the Saviour See the Father? Christ, Salvation and the Vision of God*, Bloomsbury T&T Clark, 2015.
23 F Turretin, *Institutes of Elenctic Theology*, vol 2, P&R Publishing, 1994, p 351.

and is seated at the right of God in his exaltation. Christ couldn't have the beatific vision in his humiliation.

The Reformers weren't ready to say they shared Christ with Roman Catholics without reservation, and for good reason. We'll conclude our reflections here by answering two questions that will help us to see how our differences play out.

How is Christ like us?

Roman Catholics and evangelicals both confess with Nicaea that the Son "became human", but does each group mean precisely the same thing? Do we mean the same thing when we say, "Although he was a Son, he learned obedience through what he suffered?" (Heb 5:8, ESV). Evangelicals look to Christ as an example of faith and hope. The traditional Roman Catholic doctrine of Christ's beatific vision means that Christ didn't really have either virtue. Evangelicals affirm that Christ, as our substitute, felt what we deserved to feel. He became a curse for us (Gal 3:13), feeling the wrath of God in his body *and* whole soul (Isa 53:11). Roman Catholic Christology doesn't need a Christ who was able to feel the wrath of God in this way because that's not how they believe salvation was accomplished.

Where is Christ now?

Both Roman Catholics and evangelicals would confess with the creed that the Son "ascended to heaven and is seated at the right hand of the Father". However, the real substance of their Christology expresses itself in their ecclesiology. What we really believe about Christ is what we live out in the body of Christ, the Church.

The Catholic emphasis on union

The Roman Catholic emphasis on the *union* of Christ's two natures parallels their articulation of the nature of the Church. Catholic teaching explicitly makes this connection to explain that the earthly church led by the pope and the heavenly mystical body of Christ cannot be considered as two realities, "rather they form one complex reality which coalesces from a divine and a human element".[24]

This union of the human and divine is evident in the priest's role as an *alter Christus*, another Christ,[25] who possesses Christ's "sacred power" (CCC 1551).[26] Further, the pope is an infallible ('divine') and human head of the Church who appropriates titles only fitting for the true God-man such as "pastor of the entire Church" (CCC 882).

The Lord's divine prerogative to be gracious to whom he will be gracious is delimited by the man-made

---

24 *Lumen gentium* 8. (*Lumen gentium*, the 'Dogmatic Constitution on the Church', is one of the principal documents of the Second Vatican Council from 1964. It can be accessed on the website of the Holy See: www.vatican.va/archive/hist_councils/ii_vatican_council/documents/vat-ii_const_19641121_lumen-gentium_en.html)

25 Pope Pius XI, '*Ad Catholici Sacerdotii*: Encyclical of Pope Pius Xi on the Catholic Priesthood', para 12 (www.vatican.va/content/pius-xi/en/encyclicals/documents/hf_p-xi_enc_19351220_ad-catholici-sacerdotii.html).

26 All references to the Catechism of the Catholic Church (CCC) can be found at www.vatican.va/archive/ENG0015/_INDEX.HTM. The number following 'CCC' refers to the paragraph being quoted.

structures of the Roman Catholic sacramental system, whereby God is said to work through the Church's seven sacraments to dispense the fruits of Christ's death and resurrection. Clearly, this is another problem that comes from intermingling of the divine and human aspects of the Church.

Finally, and perhaps most palpably, there is in the Eucharist "a substantial presence by which Christ, God and man, makes himself wholly and entirely present" (CCC 1374). Because of the union of the two natures, Christ must be present in his humanity (body and blood). This then creates questions for the reality of Christ's humanity. How can Christ's body and blood be present in the Eucharist at every Catholic Mass if he can only be bodily present in one place at a time?

The evangelical emphasis on distinction

The Reformed evangelical emphasis on the *distinction* between Christ's human and divine natures parallels the distinction between the visible and invisible church. No expression of the visible church, which is instituted by people on earth, can be said to perfectly reflect the invisible church which is made up of every person chosen by the Father, redeemed by the Son and indwelt by the Spirit.

The word of God, the only book inspired by the Spirit, is divine and therefore infallible but every ecclesiastical structure—no matter how large or long-standing—is human and therefore capable of error and corruption. Christ's humanity is in heaven but there is no need for a human head on earth because Christ is present with his people by the Spirit (John 14:16–17). This also means that Jesus can't be bodily present in the Lord's Supper; instead, he is spiritually present by faith.

While Roman Catholics and Reformed evangelicals both confess "one Lord Jesus Christ" they don't necessarily have the same Jesus in mind on some key points. We can see this clearly in the different answers that come from the questions we posed above: "How is Christ like us?" and "Where is he now?"

These differences are not insignificant. We need to talk about them openly and respectfully. The glory of the person of Christ as divinely revealed in the Scriptures and articulated at Nicaea compels us to do no less.

Bible study

Read John 1:1–18.

1. How does John describe the person of Christ?

2. How does John describe the Son's relationship with the Father?

3. How does John's understanding of Christ fit with the Nicene Creed?

4. How is our understanding of the person of Christ connected to our understanding of his work in salvation?

5

THE WORK OF JESUS CHRIST

Robbie Bellis

For us and for our salvation
he came down from heaven;
he became incarnate by the Holy Spirit and the
virgin Mary,
and was made human.
He was crucified for us under Pontius Pilate;
he suffered and was buried.
The third day he rose again, according to the Scriptures.
He ascended to heaven
and is seated at the right hand of the Father.

Koen, a Belgian man in his forties, started attending our evangelical church in Brussels. He was a devoted Catholic and was active in his parish, attending not only the Eucharist, but also Catholic small-group Bible studies. He came to our church having been invited by a friend and was hungry to learn more of what the Bible taught.

He listened over the next few months as we explained to him the gospel of grace. Slowly, he started to see the differences between what the Roman Catholic Church taught and what he was discovering in the Bible.

Wonderfully, after about two years, he repented and believed in Christ and was baptized as an evangelical Christian. In a telling comment, he described to me how in the Catholic Church he had been taught what it meant for Jesus to be his Lord, but he had not been clearly taught what it meant for Jesus to be his Saviour, the one who died in his place facing the judgement that we rightly deserve for our sins.

This chapter explores how Roman Catholics and evangelicals respectively understand the Nicene Creed's affirmations of Christ's work on the cross as our Saviour.

For us and for our salvation

After having expounded and defended the full divinity of God the Son, the Nicene Creed proceeds with an explanation of the doctrine of the incarnation. Why did God the Son take on flesh? The answer given is "for us and for our salvation". Salvation is the aim of the incarnation. As Kevin DeYoung points out, "if 'one substance with the Father' is the heart of the Creed, then this statement, 'who for us and for our salvation' is the beating of that heart".[1]

1   K DeYoung, 'The Nicene Creed: "For Us" and Filioque', Christ Covenant Church, *YouTube*, 21 January 2024, viewed 13 June 2024 (clearlyreformed. org/sermon/the-nicene-creed-for-us-and-filioque).

The writers of the creed frame the incarnation, crucifixion and suffering of the God-man, Christ, within the context of God's salvation plan for humanity. On this point, evangelicals and Catholics are agreed, as we see in this statement in the Catechism of the Catholic Church: "his redemptive passion was the very reason for his Incarnation" (CCC 607).[2]

He was made human and was crucified for us under Pontius Pilate

Having outlined the saving intention of God in the incarnation, the creed then goes on to describe the events of salvation: "He came down from heaven; he became incarnate by the Holy Spirit and the virgin Mary, and was made human. He was crucified for us under Pontius Pilate." What do we learn here about Christ's death, and how is this event understood by evangelicals and Catholics respectively?

Both Catholics and evangelicals agree that Christ's death is a historical event, something that the creed affirms clearly by situating Christ's crucifixion "under Pontius Pilate". Both Catholic and evangelical theologies understand Christ's work as an objective atonement made for sins. But what exactly did Christ achieve through his death on the cross? The creed's formulation that Christ was crucified "for us" summarizes the New Testament's teaching of the substitutionary nature of Christ's death.

2 All references to the Catechism of the Catholic Church (CCC) can be found at www.vatican.va/archive/ENG0015/_INDEX.HTM. The number following 'CCC' refers to the paragraph being quoted.

Indeed, the New Testament goes further than the creed in explaining the reason why Christ substituted himself for us. In 1 Corinthians, Paul outlines what the gospel is and at the heart of his summary we find an explanation of the substitutionary death of Christ: "For what I received I passed on to you as of first importance: that Christ died for our sins according to the Scriptures" (15:3). Christ's substitution is "for our sins". He died in the place of our sins. The wages of sin are death and to save us from that spiritual death, Christ died "for our sins".

He suffered and was buried

The creed then affirms that Christ suffered when he was crucified under Pontius Pilate. The question is, what did Christ suffer on the cross? The evangelical believes that Christ suffered God's curse for us. As Paul says in Galatians 3 (quoting Deuteronomy 21:23), "Christ redeemed us from the curse of the law by becoming a curse for us, for it is written, 'Cursed is everyone who is hung on a pole'" (v 13). Paul saw in Christ's crucifixion not only the opposition of sinful man, but supremely Christ bearing God's judgement against sin. Christ became the curse for us on the cross.[3]

In 2 Corinthians, Paul says that "God made him who had no sin to be sin for us, so that in him we might become the righteousness of God" (5:21). On the cross,

---

3   This is perhaps why the writers of the creed specified that Christ was "crucified for us under Pontius Pilate". The cross is the place of the divine curse.

Christ became sin—that is, like the sin-offerings in the Old Testament law, our sins were transferred to him. He was punished as if he himself had sinned. He bore our sins and faced God's curse and judgement in our place. Jesus trembled in the Garden of Gethsemane at the thought of his impending death which he described as drinking the cup (Mark 14:32–35). This cup is best understood as the cup of God's wrath and punishment that we see in the Old Testament (e.g. Jer 25:15).

What Christ suffered on the cross was no less than the punishment from God that our sins deserve. Jesus' death was therefore not only a substitution, it was a penal substitution. That is, he bore the penalty that our sins deserved in our place. This understanding of penal substitution is a core evangelical belief and is the clear teaching of both the Old and the New Testaments. Penal substitution has been believed throughout the history of the church and interestingly was also a belief held by Athanasius, one of the major influences on the Nicene Creed, who wrote:

> Formerly the world, as guilty, was under judgment from the Law; but now the Word has taken on Himself the judgment, and having suffered in the body for all, has bestowed salvation to all.[4]

4 Athanasius, *Against the Arians*, in P Schaff (ed), *Nicene and Post-Nicene Fathers*, series 2, vol 4, Eerdmans, 1975, p 341. For more on penal substitution in Athanasius' thinking, see S Jeffrey, M Ovey and A Sach, *Pierced for our Transgressions: Rediscovering the Glory of Penal Substitution*, IVP, 1994, pp 169–173 and G Williams 'Penal Substitutionary Atonement in the Church Fathers', *Evangelical Quarterly*, 2011, 8(3):203–210.

The Catholic Catechism comes close to affirming penal substitution

The 1992 Catechism of the Catholic Church (CCC) affirms that Christ died as a substitute for sinners. Quoting Isaiah 53:10–12, it states that "By his obedience to death, Jesus accomplished the substitution of the suffering Servant, who 'makes himself an *offering for sin*,' when 'he bore the sin of many', and who 'shall make many to be accounted righteous', for 'he shall bear their iniquities'" (CCC 615).

Here we have clear affirmations of Christ bearing our sin and dying as a substitute for sinners. This is much clearer language than is used in the Council of Trent, the Vatican II documents and in almost all other Roman Catholic pronouncements on the death of Christ. As evangelicals, we should make the most of this teaching and ask our Roman Catholic friends whether they really believe that Jesus died as a substitute for sinners.

It is, however, less clear whether the catechism teaches that Christ's death is a *penal* substitution. That is, did Christ bear in himself the judgement of God that we as sinners deserved so that we need never face that judgement ourselves? When the catechism explains 2 Corinthians 5:21, a classic text teaching Christ's penal substitutionary death, we read the following:

> Man's sins, following on original sin, are punishable by death. By sending his own Son in the form of a slave, in the form of a fallen humanity and [destined for death] on account of sin, God

"made him to be sin who knew no sin, so that in him we might become the righteousness of God". (CCC 602)[5]

Here, it seems that the Catholic Church understands the punishment that Christ bore on the cross as only being the fact that he took on a human nature that was "in the form of a fallen humanity and destined for death on account of sin". This stops short of the biblical witness concerning Christ's death. Christ does not only bear punishment in a general sense because he took on a human nature that was going to die, rather he specifically chose to substitute himself for sinners and to drink the cup of God's wrath in our place, bearing the punishment that we deserve.

It is therefore not surprising to read in the next paragraph of the catechism that "Jesus did not experience reprobation as if he himself had sinned" (CCC 603). It is of course true that Jesus did not despair or rebel against God as he experienced the reprobation of bearing God's wrath on the cross. However, the Bible teaches that Christ took upon himself our sin, our guilt and the punishment that we deserve for our sins. It is striking that this section of the catechism quotes many different verses from Isaiah 53 but *not* the verses at the heart of the chapter which describe Christ's substitutionary death bearing our sin, guilt and punishment:

5   Strangely, the words in square brackets are present in the Latin original (*et morti destinatae*) but not in the English translation of the catechism.

Surely he took up our pain
and bore our suffering,
yet we considered him punished by God,
stricken by him, and afflicted.
But he was pierced for our transgressions,
he was crushed for our iniquities;
the punishment that brought us peace was on him,
and by his wounds we are healed.
We all, like sheep, have gone astray,
each of us has turned to our own way;
and the Lord has laid on him
the iniquity of us all. (Isa 53:4–6)

The CCC comes close to affirming Christ's penal substitutionary death, but ultimately stops short. Let's explore this question with our Catholic friends, asking them why they believe that Jesus had to die on the cross and what they believe he achieved through his death.

Do Catholics believe in Christ's penal substitutionary death?

The French systematic theologian Henri Blocher assesses the situation in the Roman Catholic Church in this way:

Until the middle of the twentieth century, Roman Catholics also commonly held penal substitution as one element in complex theologies. In the wake of Socinian attacks, Protestant liberalism and Catholic modernism rejected objective theories, especially penal substitution ... In the

Roman Church … few scholars of note, if any, have maintained it.[6]

According to Blocher, very few modern Catholic scholars maintain belief in penal substitution. To give one example of this rejection of the doctrine, here is an extract from the report of the Vatican's official International Theological Commission on the doctrine of redemption, which explains contemporary understandings of Christ's death:

> The death of Jesus, which results inevitably from his courageous opposition to human sin, constitutes his supreme act of sacrificial self-giving, and is under that aspect pleasing to the Father, satisfying in an eminent way for the disorder of sin. Without being personally guilty or being punished by God for the sins of others, Jesus lovingly identifies with sinful humanity and experiences the pain of its alienation from God.[7]

These theologians specifically deny that Christ was being "punished by God for the sins of others" which is exactly what Isaiah 53 and the other texts above teach. They then reference paragraph 603 of the CCC which starts with the phrase, "Jesus did not experience reprobation as if he himself had sinned". This shows that leading Roman Catholic theologians understand the

---

6 H Blocher, 'Atonement', in K Vanhoozer (ed), *Dictionary for Theological Interpretation of the Bible*, Baker, 2005, pp 73–74.

7 'Select Questions on the Theology of God the Redeemer', *The Holy See*, 1995, point 39 (www.vatican.va/roman_curia/congregations/cfaith/cti_documents/rc_cti_1995_teologia-redenzione_en.html).

catechism to deny that Jesus was in any way "punished by God for the sins of others".

This Catholic understanding of Jesus' death is that he so identifies with sinful humanity that he experiences our alienation from God. When he died, the God-man did not bear God's wrath in the place of sinners, but he came alongside us in love, offering himself up to pay for our sins by his love, not by taking upon him God's just judgement that we deserve.[8] For Roman Catholicism, the death of Christ is important. Indeed, it is essential. But they do not share the biblical understanding of *why* Jesus had to die. It seems that the official position of the Roman Catholic Church is to deny Penal Substitutionary Atonement. Some Roman Catholics may believe that Christ died in our place, bearing the punishment that we deserve, but others do not.

The consequences of Christ's penal substitutionary death

One reason for the modern Roman Catholic move away from penal substitution are the logical, biblical

---

8 Historically, this is consistent with Anselm's understanding of Christ's death as a vicarious satisfaction which is not the same as the Bible and the Reformers' understanding of Christ's death as a penal substitute. Anselm famously believed that atonement (satisfaction) and punishment were distinct alternatives saying that "it is a necessary consequence, therefore, that either the honour which has been taken away should be repaid, or punishment should follow". For Anselm, by dying on the cross, Christ repaid in our place the honour that God deserves but not by facing the punishment that we deserve, which is what the Bible teaches. See Anselm of Canterbury, *Why God Became Man*, Oxford University Press, 1998, section 1:13, p 287.

implications of this doctrine. Stanislas Lyonnet and Léopold Sabourin, key critics in this area, articulate the repercussions of believing in Christ's penal substitutionary death: "If such is the truth, if our sins are imputed to Christ, then our satisfaction becomes useless".[9] In this context, "our satisfaction" refers to the works of penance which, in the Roman Catholic system, contribute to our salvation. Lyonnet and Sabourin argue that for Catholics, "the sole sufficiency of Christ's satisfaction [atoning work] does not suppress but renders possible man's own atoning contribution".[10] The language of "man's own atoning contribution" is telling, but not surprising. According to the Catholic Church, we must cooperate with God and make some contribution to our own salvation.

Jean Rivière, a renowned Catholic atonement specialist, explains that the doctrine of penal substitution "logically entails rejecting first the necessity of works of penance and also the need of Purgatory because that is designed to be the place where we accomplish the satisfaction that is still due because of our sin".[11] This approach, of course, starts not with Scripture, but with the Roman Catholic understanding of penance and

9 Lyonnet and Sabourin, *Sin, Redemption and Sacrifice: A Biblical and Patristic Study*, Biblical Institute Press, 1970, p 232.

10 Lyonnet and Sabourin, *Sin, Redemption and Sacrifice*, p 232. 'Satisfaction' is a term in theology to describe Christ's atoning work. The definition of the term depends on who is using it. Lyonnet and Sabourin believe in Anselm's definition of satisfaction, that Christ by his death satisfies God's honour, but doesn't take God's punishment on him.

11 Rivière, *Le Dogme de La Rédemption; Étude Théologique*, J Gabalda, 1931, pp 527–528.

purgatory. This leads to rejecting the clear teaching of Scripture on Christ's death on the cross.

Understanding that Christ died in our place, exhausting God's punishment that we deserve, has numerous glorious consequences for believers and undermines Catholic teaching on salvation in several ways.[12]

Firstly, Christ's penal substitutionary death goes hand in hand with the doctrine of justification by faith alone.[13] If Christ has fully paid for all our sins by dying in our place, then God can declare us righteous independent of our works. We neither merit our salvation nor cooperate with God to be saved. Christ has paid it all. It is because God condemned sin in the flesh of Christ (Rom 8:3) that there is now no more condemnation for those in Christ Jesus (Rom 8:1). The Catholic Church wrongly continues to teach that justification is a process, started at baptism, fuelled by the infusion of grace through the other sacraments, and completed by our meritorious good works. Any agreement on justification between Catholics and Protestants that does not adequately address the different understandings of what Christ achieved on the cross will remain either a purely superficial agreement, secured by using terminology which means different

12 Christ's penal substitutionary death also shows us the reality of God's wrath towards sin, a doctrine which is increasingly downplayed in the Roman Catholic Church.
13 So much so that some Catholic scholars even wrongly accuse the Reformers of inventing the doctrine of Christ's penal substitutionary death to provide the foundation for their belief in justification by faith alone.

things to each side, or a compromise on the evangelical side. The doctrine of penal substitution has a greater role to play in future discussions on justification in Catholic-Protestant dialogue.

Secondly, Christ's objective bearing of God's wrath through his substitution of himself in our place is to be appropriated by our trust, and not by the sacraments of the Catholic Church, as is the official Catholic doctrine. Christ's death means we can be saved by faith alone, not by sacramental participation.[14]

Thirdly, Christ's once for all penal substitutionary death is undermined by the blurring of the time distinctions in the Catholic Eucharist. The creed states that on the third day, Jesus "rose again, according to the Scriptures. He ascended to heaven and is seated at the right hand of the Father." The evangelical understands Christ's resurrection and ascension to the Father's side as indicating the once-for-all nature of Christ's death. His once-for-all sacrifice for sins has been accomplished. However, in Roman Catholic theology, this once-for-all nature is obscured and blurred by the re-presenting of Christ's sacrifice which is offered in the Mass.[15]

---

14 See C Kannard's chapter in this volume for an explanation of the sacramental view of salvation in the Roman Catholic Church.

15 See L De Chirico, 'The Blurring of Time Distinctions in Roman Catholicism', *Themelios*, 2002, 29(2) (thegospelcoalition.org/themelios/article/the-blurring-of-time-distinctions-in-roman-catholicism/).

Proclaiming Christ crucified

Both evangelicals and Roman Catholics recite the creed's proclamation of the saving work of Christ on the cross. However, the evangelical and biblical understanding of Christ's death as a penal substitute is not clearly affirmed in Roman Catholicism and is rejected by some, perhaps many, Catholic theologians and believers. Belief in penal substitution undermines the Roman Catholic doctrine of salvation through human cooperation with God's grace and its understanding of justification as a process involving infused righteousness and human merit.

If our Catholic friends do believe in Christ's penal substitutionary death, exploring the implications of this truth with them is a very useful way of exposing Roman Catholicism's unbiblical account of salvation. However, we must not assume that our Catholic friends who recite the words of the Nicene Creed truly understand why Christ died on the cross. We must follow Paul's example as we speak to them and preach "Jesus Christ and him crucified" (1 Cor 2:2), explaining the true meaning of Christ's death as a penal substitution for our sins.

Questions for reflection or discussion

Read Isaiah 53.

1. What do we learn about the identity of the Saviour?

2. What do we learn about the purpose of his death? Why is this good news for us?

3. What would this passage say to someone who thought they had to trust (at least in part) in their works or in the church's sacraments to be saved?

4. How could you share this good news with your Catholic friends?

6
THE HOLY SPIRIT

Gregg R. Allison

We believe in the Holy Spirit,
the Lord, the giver of life.
He proceeds from the Father and the Son,
and with the Father and the Son is worshipped and
glorified.
He spoke through the prophets.[1]

In modern times, there is much confusion about the person and work of the Holy Spirit. For some, he is almost identified with his power, credited with strange manifestations (slaying, barking), and invoked for suspect personal guidance ("the Spirit told me to do ..."). Others neglect him out of fear of such excesses and are accused of replacing the Spirit with Scripture (God is

---

1 This part of the creed includes a substantial expansion of the Nicene Creed of 325 (which succinctly affirmed belief "in the Holy Spirit") and includes the addition of the clause "and the Son" (Latin: *filioque*) from the Synod of Toledo, Spain, in 589.

"Father, Son and Holy Bible"). To some he is known as 'the Forgotten God'.[2]

How fitting it is, then, to come to this article in the Nicene Creed at this moment in time. Here we find that the church's confession of the Holy Spirit, in line with Scripture, has a firm foundation in this creedal affirmation.

Three affirmations about the Holy Spirit

The creed emphasizes three points about the Spirit.

1. The Holy Spirit is God

The creed affirms the true and full deity of the Holy Spirit, whom it names "the Lord", a divine title (in accordance with 2 Corinthians 3:17–18), and who it confesses is to be the object (together with the Father and the Son) of the church's worship and adoration. God alone can be worshipped and glorified, and the creed's affirmation expresses that the Holy Spirit is God.

2. The Holy Spirit is a divine Person

The creed confesses that he is the third person of the Trinity, proceeding from both the person who is the Father and the person who is the Son. Such eternal procession does not mean that the Spirit was created by the Father and the Son. Neither does it mean that the Spirit borrows deity from the other two persons; on the

2 See F Chan, *Forgotten God: Reversing Our Tragic Neglect of the Holy Spirit*, David C. Cook, 2009.

contrary, he is God of himself. Eternal procession means, instead, that the first person and the second person grant the third person his person of the Holy Spirit, which distinguishes the Spirit from the Father and the Son.[3] There is both strong biblical support for this affirmation (John 14:26, 15:26, 16:7; Acts 2:33; Rom 8:9) and a robust theological case for it.[4] This double procession of the Holy Spirit is the confession of the Western churches—i.e. Roman Catholic and Protestant churches—and is denied by Eastern Orthodox churches.[5]

3. The Holy Spirit engages in divine works

This article in the creed focuses on two major works in which the Spirit (always working together with the Father and the Son) is involved.

---

3 For further discussion see GR Allison and AJ Köstenberger, *The Holy Spirit*, B&H Academic, 2020, chapters 14–15.

4 Augustine explained the double procession of the Spirit from both the Father and the Son: "It is not to no purpose that in this Trinity the Son and none other is called the Word of God, and the Holy Spirit and none other is called the Gift of God, and God the Father alone is he from whom the Word is born [begotten or generated], and from whom the Holy Spirit principally proceeds. And therefore I have added the word principally, because we find that the Holy Spirit proceeds from the Son also. But the Father gave [the Son] this too, not as to one already existing, and not yet having it; but whatever he gave to the only-begotten Word, he gave by begetting him. Therefore he so begat him as that the common Gift should proceed from him also, and the Holy Spirit should be the Spirit of both." Augustine, *On the Trinity*, book 15, chapter 17, section 29 in P Schaff (ed), *Nicene and Post-Nicene Fathers*, series 1, vol 3, p 216; cf. T Aquinas, *Summa Theologica*, part 1, question 36, art. 2–3.

5 For further discussion see M Levering, *Engaging the Doctrine of the Holy Spirit: Love and Gift in the Trinity and the Church*, Baker Academic, 2016, chapters 2–3.

First, he is the "giver of life" in both the works of creation (Gen 1:2; Ps 33:6) and re-creation through conviction of sin (John 16:8–11), regeneration (John 3:1–8), sanctification (2 Thess 2:13) and glorification (Rom 8:11). Second, he "spoke through the prophets" in as the author of divine revelation, with particular reference to written Scripture (2 Tim 3:16; 2 Pet 1:16–21). These key areas of work are among many other mighty works attributed to the Spirit—for example, his filling of the incarnate Son "without limit" (John 3:34) and his distribution of spiritual gifts to the church (1 Cor 12:7, 11)—and underscore the truth of the Spirit's divine personhood.

As noted above, Roman Catholic and Protestant theology, over against Eastern Orthodox theology, affirm that the Holy Spirit proceeds from the Father and the Son. This doctrine cements theological agreement among the first two major branches of Christendom and grounds the division between them and the third branch. Indeed, Protestantism draws its belief about this double procession not only from Scripture, which is its ultimate authority in all such matters, but also from the doctrinal tradition it inherited from Roman Catholicism. Of course, affirmations of other aspects of the person and work of the Holy Spirit find common agreement among all three branches.

Two significant differences about the Holy Spirit

Along with this important harmony, substantive differences contribute to an ongoing division between the Roman Catholic and Protestant traditions. Perhaps the most obvious disagreement concerns the Holy Spirit's work in the leadership and rites of the Roman Catholic Church. Given that chapter 8 of this book will cover the doctrine of the church in general, my focus will be on two specific areas: the priesthood and the sacraments.

The priesthood

According to Roman Catholic doctrine, Jesus Christ established the priesthood in his promise to Peter to build the church on him and to give him the keys of the kingdom (Matt 16:13–20). Moreover, the consecration and empowerment for this priestly ministry was conferred on the apostles through Jesus' impartation of the Holy Spirit (John 20:21–23).

This ordination and enablement continue through the sacrament of Holy Orders. Christ endowed his apostles with a special outpouring of the Holy Spirit, and they in turn transmitted to the successors—the bishops—the gift of the Spirit through the laying on of hands. The same practice continues up to this day through episcopal [priestly] consecration.[6]

This act is the sacrament of Holy Orders, which "confers a gift of the Holy Spirit that permits the exercise of a 'sacred power' (*sacra potestas*) which can come only from Christ himself through his Church" (CCC 1538).[7] This gift is the grace of the Holy Spirit

6 For more on this, see my book *Roman Catholic Theology and Practice: An Evangelical Assessment*, Crossway, 2014, p 360.
7 All references to the Catechism of the Catholic Church (CCC) can be found at www.vatican.va/archive/ENG0015/_INDEX.HTM. The number following 'CCC' refers to the paragraph being quoted.

by which these ordained men possess an indelible mark, rendering them a different essence from all other human beings.

This mark is vividly portrayed and conferred by the anointing of these men with consecrated oil, which is "a sign of the special anointing of the Holy Spirit who makes their ministry fruitful" (CCC 1574). As appropriately consecrated priests, they possess the needed resources to act 'in the person of Christ' (*in persona Christi*) as they engage in the ministries of teaching, ruling and sanctifying the laity in the Roman Catholic Church.[8] Thus, the Holy Spirit is thoroughly responsible for the existence and ministry of the Roman Catholic priesthood.

The sacraments

This last arena of priestly responsibility—the sanctification of the faithful—introduces my second main point: the sacraments, which are the principal means of sanctification for the Catholic faithful. The Church has seven sacraments: "Baptism, Confirmation or Chrismation, Eucharist, Penance, Anointing of the Sick, Holy Orders, and Matrimony" (CCC 1113). It considers these to be "actions of the Holy Spirit" operating in the Church (CCC 1116). Furthermore, as sacraments of the Church, they are both "by her" (i.e. the Catholic Church) and "for her". The sacraments are "by her" because the

---

8 Three degrees of Holy Orders are present in the Church: the episcopate (for bishops), the presbyterate (for priests), and the diaconate (for deacons).

Church "is the sacrament of Christ's action at work in her through the mission of the Holy Spirit" (CCC 1118). They are "for her" in that "the sacraments make the Church" by fostering communion with the triune God through the actions of its priests (CCC 1118).

From the Roman Catholic Church as the sacrament of Christ's work through the Holy Spirit's work, flow the seven sacraments, each of which is thoroughly tied to the Spirit.

Baptism
"Holy Baptism is the basis of the whole Christian life, the gateway to life in the Spirit ... and the door which gives access to the other sacraments" (CCC 1213). Specifically, "through the Holy Spirit, Baptism is a bath that purifies, justifies, and sanctifies" (CCC 1227), which means that baptism is necessary for salvation.

Confirmation
"By the sacrament of Confirmation, [the baptized] are more perfectly bound to the Church and are enriched with a special strength of the Holy Spirit" (CCC 1285). Specifically, "the sacrament of Confirmation is conferred through the anointing with chrism [consecrated oil] on the forehead, which is done by the laying on of hands, and through the words ... ['Be sealed with the Gift of the Holy Spirit']" (CCC 1300).

Eucharist
This third sacrament is "the source and summit of the Christian life" because the "whole spiritual good of

the Church, namely Christ himself", is present in the Eucharist (CCC 1324). As to its view of the presence of Christ in this sacrament, Roman Catholic theology holds to transubstantiation: "At the heart of the Eucharistic celebration are the bread and wine that, by the words of Christ and the invocation of the Holy Spirit, become Christ's Body and Blood" (CCC 1333). As the priest recites Jesus' words from the Last Supper (Matt 26:26–28) and prays for God the Father to send the Holy Spirit, the natural elements of bread and wine are transformed into the sacrament of the Eucharist, saving and sanctifying its recipients through the infusion of grace.

Penance

This sacrament is designed "for all sinful members of [Christ's] Church: above all for those who, since Baptism, have fallen into grave sin, and have thus lost their baptismal grace and wounded ecclesial communion"—that is, fellowship with the Roman Catholic Church (CCC 1446). As a new possibility for members who have lost their salvation "to convert and to recover the grace of justification" (CCC 1446), this sacrament depends on the Holy Spirit to convict of sin and prompt toward conversion (CCC 1989, 1993).

Anointing of the sick

By this sacrament, "the whole Church commends those who are ill to the suffering and glorified Lord, that he may raise them up and save them" (CCC 1499). Through this anointing, the Holy Spirit gives grace to renew trust in God and to strengthen the resolve of the sick and dying not to fall into Satanic temptation and despair as they approach death.

Matrimony

This sacrament initiates and seals a marital covenant between a husband and wife. It is prepared for by the sacrament of penance, mutually conferred upon each other, and celebrated with the sacrament of the Eucharist. Like all sacraments, matrimony confers a special grace upon the couple and, as such, involves the work of the Holy Spirit to establish a permanent, indissoluble bond between husband and wife and to perfect their love (CCC 1641).

Holy orders

We've already discussed this sacrament under the heading, 'The priesthood'.

We can clearly see that for the Roman Catholic Church, the Holy Spirit is engaged in the consecration and empowerment of the priesthood, which in turn is engaged in the administration of the seven sacraments. These visible signs, through the operation of the Spirit, impart invisible grace that transforms the very nature of the Catholic faithful, enabling them to engage in good works and thus merit eternal life.[9]

9   This definition of a sacrament comes from Augustine, *On the Catechizing of the Uninstructed*, chapter 26, section 50, in P Schaff (ed), *Nicene and Post-Nicene Fathers of the Christian Church*, series 1, vol 3, Hendrickson, 1994, p 312.

An evangelical doctrine of the Holy Spirit

An evangelical doctrine of the Holy Spirit with respect to the priesthood and the sacraments is significantly different from the Roman Catholic version. It centres on the Protestant view of the priesthood of all believers. This doctrine maintains that all Christians stand before God through the High Priest Jesus Christ (Heb 2:14–18, 4:14–16) and without the mediation of any others. It also means that all church members are divinely appointed and empowered to minister to one another.

The priesthood of all believers

Through the decisive, covenant-changing work of the High Priest Jesus Christ (Heb 7:23–28), a new and better priesthood has been inaugurated. Indeed, it has replaced the old covenant and its priesthood, which was reserved for men from the tribes of Aaron and Levi. In this new covenant, Christ has made his followers—*all* his followers—"a kingdom and priests to serve his God and Father" (Rev 1:6; cf. 5:9–10). Peter addresses this priesthood of all believers:

> As you come to him, the living Stone—rejected by humans but chosen by God and precious to him—you also, like living stones, are being built into a spiritual house to be a holy priesthood, offering spiritual sacrifices acceptable to God through Jesus Christ. (1 Pet 2:4–5)

What are these "spiritual sacrifices" that we royal priests offer? According to the New Testament, we are to:

- offer our bodies and ourselves as living sacrifices, holy and pleasing to God—this is our true worship (Rom 12:1)
- give worshipful expressions of praise and thanksgiving to the Lord (Heb 13:15) as both individual believers and when gathered together as the church
- perform acts of service and physical provisions for others (Heb 13:16)—we engage in good works and give financial support for our church and its many ministries
- partner in the ministry of the gospel (Phil 1:5, 4:15)—we provide resources for the advancement of the gospel
- encourage conversions to Christ—we lead others to faith through the announcement of the gospel (Rom 15:16–17)
- "consider how we may spur one another on toward love and good deeds" as we gather for worship (Heb 10:24), because we "have confidence to enter the Most Holy Place by the blood of Jesus" (v 19) and because we "have a great priest over the house of God" (v 21).

Finally, should God call us, we may offer the greatest spiritual sacrifice by being "poured out like a drink offering"—that is, martyrdom (Phil 2:17; 2 Tim 4:6).

In sum, the essential purpose of the royal priesthood of believers is that we would declare "the praises of him who called you out of darkness into his wonderful light" (1 Pet 2:9; cf. Col 3:16).

This doctrine of the priesthood of all believers was first articulated by Martin Luther and affirmed by the other leading Reformers. It critiqued and sought to dismantle the Roman Catholic Church's exaltation of its priesthood above the laity. It insisted instead on the equality of all Christians rather than a hierarchy based on an essential difference between priests and lay people.

This doctrine still affirms the necessity of the office of ministry for church leaders who are called and equipped by the Holy Spirit to teach, lead, pray and shepherd churches. At the same time, it upholds the privilege and empowerment of all church members to minister as royal priests through the Spirit's power and gifts (1 Cor 12:7, 11).[10]

The sacraments

A second point of difference concerns the sacraments and their role in the salvation and sanctification of God's people. A major divide between Roman Catholicism and Protestantism is the number of these rites: seven for the Catholic Church, two for Protestant churches. This divergence means that evangelical churches do not believe that the Holy Spirit consecrates, operates through, and confers grace through the Catholic

10 Protestant denominations like Anglicanism and Episcopalianism refer to their church leaders as priests, but the majority of Protestant churches do not use this title. One reason is to distance themselves from the Roman Catholic Church's priesthood, in accordance with the early Reformers rejection of it. Common terms for such leaders in these churches are pastors, elders, ministers, bishops, presbyters and deacons.

sacraments of confirmation, penance, anointing of the sick, holy orders and matrimony. There are only two rites to be observed in Protestant churches.

One of these is baptism. Most evangelical churches do not believe that the Holy Spirit so works through baptism that it is necessary for salvation. Rather, repentance from sin and faith in Jesus Christ (apart from all works) is all that is needed to embrace the gospel and experience redemption. So contrary to the Roman Catholic idea that justification comes through faith and baptism, evangelical churches insist that God's pronouncement that sinful people are *not guilty but righteous instead* is a declaration that makes it so.[11]

Accompanying this divine announcement are other mighty works of God: regeneration, union with Christ, adoption, assurance of salvation, sanctification —all of which come about through the Holy Spirit. For evangelical churches that baptize believers (credobaptism), baptism is a public affirmation of God's saving work in their life. For evangelical churches that baptize infants of believing members (paedobaptism), baptism is a promise of God's covenant love for those

---

11 The doctrine of justification continues to be a major point of division between Roman Catholicism and Protestantism and centres on the two traditions' definitions. For Roman Catholicism, "justification is not only the remission of sins but also the sanctification and renewal of the inner man" (CCC 1989). In other words, this view blends justification, sanctification and regeneration, and renders salvation a lifelong process. For Protestantism, justification is as I have presented it: a legal declaration by which God pronounces sinful people "not guilty but righteous instead". For further discussion, see Allison, *Roman Catholic Theology and Practice*, chapter 13.

children and a pledge of God's saving work in their life in the future. In neither case is baptism necessary for salvation. That does not mean, however, that baptism is unimportant. It is a step of obedience commanded by Jesus himself (Matt 28:19) and closely tied to the work of the Holy Spirit (e.g. Acts 2:38).

The second rite is the Lord's Supper. No Protestant church holds to transubstantiation, the Roman Catholic view of the presence of Christ in this sacrament. There is no solid biblical basis for this idea nor theological foundation for the notion that the Holy Spirit transforms the Eucharistic elements into the body and blood of Christ.

Rather, following Martin Luther, Huldrych Zwingli and John Calvin, Protestant churches affirm three different views of the Lord's Supper. One is Luther's *sacramental union* (or *consubstantiation*): Christ is truly present in both his deity and humanity, 'in, with and under' the substance of the bread and wine.

A second is Zwingli's *memorial view*: the Lord's Supper is a memorial of Christ's death in accordance with Jesus's instructions, "Do this in remembrance of me" (Luke 22:19; 1 Cor 11:24). Thus, the celebration of the Lord's Supper, as a nonverbal but vivid portrayal of Christ's sacrificial death on the cross, prompts Christians to recall that work and celebrate salvation.

The third is Calvin's *spiritual presence* view: Moving beyond the memorial view, Calvin maintained that the bread and wine are certainly symbols, but they are not empty symbols. Indeed, they render what they symbolize. By his spiritual presence, Christ presents himself and his saving benefits through these means of grace.[12]

While we can see there is room for some debate among evangelicals as to the exact nature of what happens at the Lord's Supper, each of these Reformed possibilities are very distinct from what is claimed by Roman Catholics.

Same words; different meanings

Roman Catholics and evangelicals both agree with the creed's article on the Holy Spirit. At the same time, there are significant differences between each church's doctrine on the Holy Spirit, which is clearly exemplified by the divergent views on the priesthood and the sacraments. A common confession should not mask these substantial points of disparity on this doctrine that is at the heart of what it means to be the church.

12 For more on this see my book *The Church: An Introduction*, Short Studies in Systematic Theology, Crossway, 2021, p 121.

Questions for reflection or discussion

1. Why are the different views of the sacraments so important to understand? Which is correct?

2. How do you assess your church's emphasis on (or neglect of) the Holy Spirit? What benefits does a proper emphasis bring to your church, and what drawbacks does neglect bring? If your church lacks attention to the Spirit, what steps could be taken to rectify this oversight or disregard for him?

3. As you read John chapters 14, 15 and 16, what do you find out about the person of the Holy Spirit (who he is) and the work of the Holy Spirit (what he does)?

4. As you read Romans 8, what do you find out about the importance of the presence and power of the Holy Spirit for living the Christian life?

7

THE VIRGIN MARY

Lauren J. Montenegro

[Jesus Christ] became incarnate by the holy Spirit and the virgin Mary.

As an evangelical in France, I am often asked variations of this question: "What's the difference between Roman Catholics and Protestants? You guys don't believe in the Virgin Mary, right?"

It seems to be the first thing that people notice when comparing Roman Catholics and Protestants: Roman Catholics seem to 'believe' in Mary, while evangelicals do not. Or do we? The Nicene Creed states that Jesus "became incarnate by the Holy Spirit and the virgin Mary". But today, the way that Roman Catholics and evangelicals understand this part of the creed shows that there is much more to the story than a simple statement of agreement.

The place of the virgin Mary in Roman Catholicism has developed in significance over the past 1700 years since this Nicene Creed was written. In fact, the virgin Mary was only added to the creed in 381 AD, when the creed was revised at the Council of Constantinople.[1] Since then, Roman Catholics have articulated four key beliefs, known as 'dogmas', about the mother of Jesus.[2] They are:

- *Mary as the 'Theotokos' ('God-bearer')*: the belief that Mary is the mother of God.
- *The perpetual virginity of Mary*: the belief that Mary remained a virgin before, during and after the birth of Christ.[3]
- *The immaculate conception of Mary*: the belief that Mary was conceived without the stain of original sin. (This is often misunderstood, as it is not a reference to the virgin birth of Jesus, but the belief that Mary herself was not born with original sin like the rest of humanity.)
- *The assumption of Mary*: the belief that because she was without the stain of original sin, Mary's body and soul were assumed up into heaven at the end of her earthly life, and she didn't suffer the corruption of the grave as a consequence of sin.

1 For more on this see chapter 1.
2 These were outlined clearly at the Second Vatican Council in 1964. See especially chapter 8 of *Lumen gentium*, one of the principal documents of the Second Vatican Council, which can be accessed on the website of the Holy See: www.vatican.va/archive/hist_councils/ii_vatican_council/documents/vat-ii_const_19641121_lumen-gentium_en.html.
3 To say that Mary remained a virgin *during* the birth of Christ is to say that she did not give birth naturally, but supernaturally.

What is Mariology?

Few evangelicals have even heard of Mariology—the discipline of studying the virgin Mary. Because Mary has such a significant place in Roman Catholicism, a whole field of study has developed to examine and hypothesize about what Mary's role might be in salvation history. The central premise of Mariology is that she was not fully revealed in Scripture but is being progressively revealed and discovered over time by the Roman Catholic Church.[4] For example, at the time of the writing of Scripture, Christians were not 'ready' to know about the assumption of Mary. However, by 1950, after centuries of speculation through the study of anthropology, church history and the magisterium, the Roman Catholic Church deemed that the world was ready for the proclamation of this dogma.

1700 years of Roman Catholic Mariology

Though the words of the Nicene Creed are essentially the same as they have been since 381 AD, 1700 years of spiritual practice and church history have influenced what these words mean. In Roman Catholicism, the four dogmas are clearly defined examples of how Mary's place in the creed has increased in significance.

The first two dogmas—Mary as the *Theotokos* and the perpetual virginity of Mary—were defined early

---

4 This definition is gleaned from Pontifical International Marian Academy, *The Mother of the Lord: Memory, Presence, Hope: Presenting a Review of the Actual Questions Facing Mariology Today* (St Pauls, 2007).

in church history. These ideas were already being discussed at the time of the First Council of Nicaea but were only more formally established afterwards: the *Theotokos* at the Council of Ephesus in 431, and the perpetual virginity of Mary in 553 at the Second Council of Constantinople. The latter two dogmas—the immaculate conception and the assumption of Mary— came more than a millennium later.

What is important to note about the first two dogmas is that, to some extent, their intention was good, though the outcome was ultimately detrimental to the gospel. The Council of Ephesus intended to stamp out Arianism and affirm the divinity of Christ.[5] In this way, it was necessary to articulate that the child born to Mary was God himself and not a created being. The goal was to affirm the identity of Christ as "begotten, not made". But the consequence was an unintended veneration of Mary.

Around the same era, the dogma of Mary's perpetual virginity developed simply because it seemed unthinkable that Mary had marital relations with Joseph or conceived children after giving birth to Christ. It was unimaginable that life would go on 'as normal' after giving birth to God incarnate. The perpetual virginity of Mary was contemplated and discussed for centuries by different Church Fathers before it was articulated in a council in the sixth century.

But there is another idea that contributed to the

---

5   Arianism is the idea that Jesus was the Son of God *created* by God the Father, rather than being eternal. See chapter 1 for more on this.

perpetual virginity dogma, articulated most firmly by Church Father and theologian Jerome: that virginity is superior to matrimony.[6] This teaching from Jerome not only influenced Mariology, but has also profoundly impacted Catholicism to this day, particularly as we still see the high value placed on the celibacy of priests, nuns and monks.[7]

The two early dogmas were not without their impact on the Protestant faith. Martin Luther, Thomas Cranmer, John Wycliffe and later John Wesley all held to a belief in the perpetual virginity of Mary. The *Theotokos* dogma was also widely accepted by Protestants, including Martin Luther and John Calvin, albeit with a significant disclaimer from Calvin. He argued that while the *Theotokos* title could be recognized for its theological truth—Mary *did* give birth to God incarnate and, in that sense, she was indeed the mother of God— Protestants should be wary of using this title simply because it has fed an idolatrous veneration of the virgin Mary in the Catholic Church.[8]

6 Jerome wrote his treatise *On the Perpetual Virginity of Mary against Helvidius* in 382.
7 The Reformers rejected Jerome's teaching on the superiority of virginity over matrimony and argued that it wasn't necessary for priests to remain celibate. The legacy of this thinking can be felt today in evangelical faith communities, where we have arguably swung too far in the opposite direction and run the risk of elevating the importance of marriage over singleness. It's important to notice that our evangelical reactions to Roman Catholic teaching, both positive and negative, can have a genuine impact on our own faith practice, even without our realizing it.
8 Calvin discusses this in his commentary on Luke 1:43 in *Commentary on a Harmony of the Evangelists, Matthew, Mark, and Luke*, vol 1. See also Calvin's *A Treatise on Relics*, Johnstone and Hunter, 1870 (gutenberg.org/files/32136/32136-pdf.pdf).

The latter two dogmas—the immaculate conception and the assumption of Mary—came in the 19th and 20th centuries. Despite their relatively recent recognition, they can be considered extensions (and unbiblical consequences) of the two earlier dogmas. The continual elevation of Mary's virginity, but also the use of 'Mother of God' as a title, led to the belief that for God to be born of a woman, the woman needed to have been the purest and most perfect of all women. Following on from this, it was also reasoned that the woman who gave birth to God-incarnate could not have been able to pass on original sin to her Son.

From these reflections came the dogma of the immaculate conception of Mary, which then made necessary the fourth dogma, the assumption of Mary. For if she was born without the stain of original sin, the consequence of sin—death (Rom 6:23)—would not apply to her.

What began as the belief of Mary's perpetual virginity and the declaration that she gave birth to God-incarnate progressed in Roman Catholic Mariology to the existence of two further dogmas that are far removed from biblical truth.

1700 years of popular devotion to Mary

But Mariology is more than simply the history of the dogmas. This is only a tiny part of what Mary means to Roman Catholics. Mary permeates the life of Roman Catholic believers through many experiences and practices: pilgrimages, the Rosary and apparitions of Mary also reveal that she has an active role in the spiritual lives of the Roman Catholic faithful.

More than 2,400 claims of Marian apparitions have been recorded throughout history, fewer than 20 of which are formally recognized by the Roman Catholic Church.[9] Believers often pilgrimage to the sites of her apparitions to experience a sacred place, to pray and to ask her to pray for them. The apparitions of Mary have significantly impacted the way Roman Catholics see her. She is much more than an historical figure who was born and died in the first century; she is someone to relate to, pray to, venerate and seek as a source of maternal comfort in times of need. In many cases, the believer who observes the apparition reports a promise of healing or deliverance from Mary, a request to build a shrine in her honour, or an appeal from her to pray the Rosary more frequently.[10]

The practice of praying the Rosary has been widely propagated since the 13th century. This tactile structure of prayer uses a strand of beads to help count the number of prayers made. The prayers that compose the Rosary are arranged in sets of ten 'Hail Marys' (called 'decades')— one for each of the ten small beads—and one 'Our Father' (the Lord's Prayer). The virgin Mary is prayed to ten times for every one time the Lord's Prayer is prayed.

9   Around 2,400 apparitions are recorded by René Laurentin and Patrick Sbalchiero in *Dictionnaire des "apparitions" de la Vierge Marie*, 2nd edn, Fayard, 2017. Michael O'Neill records a similar number on the Miracle Hunter website: miraclehunter.com/marian_apparitions/index.html

10 In *Dictionnaire des "apparitions" de la Vierge Marie*, Laurentin and Sblachiero report that in 184 apparition claims, Mary allegedly requested that a chapel be built.

This devotion cannot help but increase affection for the virgin Mary in Roman Catholic believers, and therefore it encourages her veneration. *Veneration* is distinct from *worship* in Roman Catholicism, which is reserved for God alone. Veneration is reserved for the honouring of saints, and the virgin Mary receives *hyper-veneration*, which is an elevated status of honour above the saints but still considered 'below' worship. In practice, however, the hyper-veneration of Mary often resembles worship.

And herein lies the challenge to unity between Catholics and evangelicals. The Nicene Creed proclaims that we believe Jesus was incarnate by the Holy Spirit and the virgin Mary, but who is this Mary? When Roman Catholics recite the creed, are they professing a belief in a Mary who is actively engaging in the world, who is to be venerated and prayed to, who was born without original sin, and who was assumed bodily into heaven. This is not the same Mary that evangelicals profess in the creed.

Scandalous evangelical Mariology

A few years ago, I found myself at a Mariology conference in France. There were many nuns, priests and Roman Catholic theologians. I was the only evangelical. As part of a discussion on Mary in film, we watched an episode of *The Chosen* featuring Mary at the wedding in Cana.[11] Most spoke positively about the episode as we discussed it, yet a passionate but unassuming French

11 Dallas Jenkins (director), 'The Wedding Gift' [television program], *The Chosen* (season 1, episode 5), Angel Studios, Utah, 2019.

THE NICENE CREED

nun seated next to me couldn't help but gently express her disappointment with how Mary was portrayed. She smiled modestly and said, "I would have liked to have seen her shine more, to be more radiant".

Many Roman Catholics also had a difficult time with the prequel to the series, where Mary experiences pain during childbirth. This is considered by some Roman Catholics, including Saint Bernard de Clairvaux, as inconsistent with the dogma of the perpetual virginity, for it is believed that Mary painlessly gave birth and remained a virgin *during* childbirth. This belief that Mary gave birth painlessly is also related to the dogma of the immaculate conception. If she was born without the stain of original sin, then she ought not to suffer sin's consequence of pain in childbirth.

On another occasion, I remember sharing my beliefs about Mary with the same nun. I sincerely tried to be kind and sensitive in my description of Mary, expressing how I found it beautiful that Mary was a simple young woman whom God had chosen for this amazing miracle. However, believing that she was just as human and imperfect as we are, just as much in need of a Saviour as we are, was far too shocking for this dear religious sister. So perturbed was she by my words that she put both hands up to her own neck and said, "You are strangling me with your words". This was the first time I encountered just how hurtful and scandalous our evangelical beliefs about Mary can seem.

While we may never mean to disrespect Mary, rejecting the elaborate Roman Catholic version of Mary can appear irreverent to both Christ and his mother. To assert that the mother of God had marital relations with Joseph and had other children is seen as sacrilegious, for the dogma of perpetual virginity insists that the body that carried the Christ remained holy and untouched. Many Roman Catholics *love* Mary and have a powerful emotional attachment to her. We need to be sensitive and aware that we are speaking of someone they consider not just the mother of Christ but also their own spiritual mother. Anything short of reverence for the virgin Mary can be regarded as offensive.

While it might seem irreverent toward Mary, evangelical Mariology centres its reverence solely on the work of Christ and his all-sufficient sacrifice. Was Mary's womb pure and worthy enough to house the one true living God? Scripture is clear that no human is pure and worthy (Rom 3:10–12) and sin has penetrated every part of us. And yet, in his humility—a humility worthy of all reverence and veneration—Christ came into this world through an imperfect woman. What a weak way for God himself to come into a broken world. This leaves me in awe. This leads me to worship. The great light of Christ came into the darkest of worlds: "I have come into the world as a light, so that no one who believes in me should stay in darkness" (John 12:46). Mary was also walking in darkness.

Meditation on the incarnation of Christ necessarily leads us to ponder Mary and her role in the story of salvation. As evangelicals, we tend to shy away from Mary, but the Nicene Creed reminds us that we do need to contemplate what it means that Jesus was incarnate by the Holy Spirit *and the virgin Mary.* The incarnation is a miracle of miracles. It is more than just the miracle of a virgin becoming pregnant, it is God becoming flesh to live among humans; it is the human being Jesus being incarnate of God himself, the Holy Spirit; it is God himself being incarnate of a human, Mary. Not only is this strikingly beautiful, but it is also deeply *loving*. For our redemption, God "made himself nothing by taking the very nature of a servant, being made in human likeness" (Phil 2:7).

The love of God the Father

For a few years, I was involved in ministry in the Marian pilgrimage city of Lourdes, France. During that time, a friend visiting from Australia told me about a conversation she'd had on a local bus with a priest. She shared with the priest that she was visiting her evangelical friend, and they started discussing prayer to the virgin Mary. The priest shared this very common analogy: if you want something from Dad, the best way to get it is to go to Mum. Mum has Dad's ear. Mum can twist Dad's arm. He said it is the same with Mary. He encouraged her to pray to the mother of God in order to receive from God the Father.

This concept only makes sense if you have an inaccessible and harsh father, a father who is not inclined to listen and needs some kind of persuasion whenever we come to him with our requests. This is not how Jesus talks about God the Father. God the Father loves to give good gifts to his children (Matt 7:11). Romans 8:15 talks about us receiving "the Spirit of adoption as sons". That means we have in us the very same Spirit from which Jesus was incarnate, by whom we are able call out "Abba, Father!" in the dependence of a child. Our God is an accessible Father with whom we can share a loving, intimate closeness. Elevating Mary as 'Mother' over all mankind does two things: it subtracts from the sufficient goodness and love of God the Father, and it promotes her, as a created being, into a role only God should have in our lives.

A way forward

Evangelicals do very much 'believe' in the virgin Mary, as she has been outlined in Scripture: a young unmarried virgin woman who miraculously conceived. We can recite the Nicene Creed confidently as we marvel at the incarnation. However, Roman Catholicism has been progressively discovering and unveiling what they believe to be true of the virgin Mary. After 1700 years of dogmas, apparitions and Rosary prayers, her portrait vastly differs from what we see in Scripture. The discrepancy between what Roman Catholics and evangelicals see in Mary is significant enough for us to question if we are making the same statement of faith when reciting the Nicene Creed.

But this should not deter us from going further. While our differences persist theologically, we are now at a time in history where, relationally, we can debate, discuss and disagree without fear of violence. For evangelicals, this means engaging with Mariology as we are led by the Scriptures, where we find Mary to be a heroine of our faith. It means contemplating in more depth the incarnation of our Lord and knowing more deeply the love of God the Father for us, his children.

Questions for reflection or discussion

1. Have you ever talked with a Roman Catholic about Mary? If you're in a group setting, share your experiences.

2. Read Luke 1:46–55. What is at the heart of Mary's prayer?

3. Read John 2:1–12. What can we learn about Mary and her relationship to Jesus in this passage?

4. Read Matthew 7:9–11. What does it mean to you that God is your Father?

8
ONE HOLY CATHOLIC AND APOSTOLIC CHURCH

Mark Gilbert

We believe in one holy catholic and apostolic church.

Even though I left the Roman Catholic Church almost 30 years ago, I still take my mother to Mass from time to time. One time, as we said these words of creed together: "We believe in the one, holy, catholic and apostolic church", I remember thinking that we actually mean different things by the words, 'we', 'believe', 'in the one', 'holy', 'catholic', 'apostolic' and 'church'— though at least we seem to agree on the meaning of the word 'and'.[1]

---

1   The Catechism of the Catholic Church 1994 (CCC) includes teaching on the one holy catholic and apostolic church, and what they call four essential features of the church, in paragraphs 811–870 (www.vatican.va/archive/ENG0015/_INDEX.HTM). Further development of these teachings can also be found in the Compendium of the Catechism of the Catholic Church 2005 (CCCC) in paragraphs 147–176 (www.vatican.va/archive/compendium_ccc/documents/archive_2005_compendium-ccc_en.html).

While these words had particular meanings for the original authors of the creed, today some of these words have come to mean quite different things for Catholics and evangelicals. I no longer say the creed in a Roman Catholic setting because I think it is unhelpful, if not dishonest, to pretend I am united with people I am in clear disagreement with. This chapter will tease out some of the original meanings of the words 'one', 'holy', 'catholic', 'apostolic' and 'church', traditionally known as the marks of the church, as well as the ways Roman Catholics and evangelicals commonly use them today.

We believe ...

Before discussing the meanings of these words, it is worth noting that Roman Catholics are called to believe, as a matter of faith, in the idea that the one holy catholic and apostolic church subsists in the Roman Catholic Church,[2] even if evidence were to suggest the contrary.[3] They are called to believe that all Christian expressions are ultimately a part of the Roman Catholic Church.

This is a circular argument: they are called to believe in the Roman Catholic Church, which teaches them to believe in the Roman Catholic Church. They are also called to rely on the Roman Catholic Church for the divine works of salvation, sanctification, infallible

---

2   As the catechism highlights, "only faith can recognize that the Church possesses these properties from her divine source" (CCC 812).

3   *Lumen gentium* 8. The Roman Catholic Church is not claiming that other elements of sanctification or truth do not exist outside the structure of the Roman Catholic Church, but that the one holy catholic and apostolic Church subsists within the Roman Catholic Church.

truth and supernatural blessings or graces through the sacraments.

This is another outworking of the 'Christ-Church interconnection'[4] or the claim that the Roman Catholic Church fails to properly distinguish between Christ and the church so that faith in Christ becomes faith in the Roman Catholic Church. The 'Christ-Church interconnection' has been raised in earlier chapters as well, as it infects many areas of Roman Catholic teaching. The Scriptures, in contrast, call Christians to put their faith in Christ alone.

One

Unity for the sake of unity? One of the main driving forces of Roman Catholicism, if not *the* driving force, is unity.[5] It is the Church's reason for being. It is the Church's identity as the visible united Church. In the catechism they put it this way: "Unity is the essence of the Church" (CCC 813). If we look at some of the statements calling for unity from Pope Francis, we can see this in practice.

Firstly, years ahead of the 1700th anniversary of Nicaea, Pope Francis was calling for all Christian denominations to use this as an opportunity to demonstrate unity. He has challenged the Orthodox churches to be

---

4 This term was coined by Gregg Allison in *Roman Catholic Theology and Practice: An Evangelical Assessment* (Crossway, 2014). See pages 56–63.
5 This point is argued by Leondardo De Chirico in *Evangelical Theological Perspectives on Post-Vatican II Roman Catholicism*, Religions and Discourse, vol 19, P Lang, 2003, p 197.

united on the date of Easter, and he has called other denominations for a demonstration of ecumenical unity around the Nicene Creed that we all profess.

These overarching calls for unity are not the first. In 2016, in the lead up to the 500th anniversary of Martin Luther publishing his 95 theses, Pope Francis claimed that Catholics and Protestants were united on the doctrine of justification—that both groups believe that we are saved by grace alone through faith.[6] This was despite the vast majority of Protestants being in profound disagreement with the Roman Catholic Church on what this means.[7] Both groups may say the same words—grace, faith, saved and alone—but they mean very different things by these words.

Christians are called to stand together in the truth of the gospel. The unity that Jesus calls for is a unity that is based on faith in the truth found in God's word (John 17:18–21). This unity, however, will at times lead to division. Jesus says this (Luke 14:26–27), so does the apostle Paul (1 Cor 11:18–19).

For Christians, unity is a reality for all those who are saved by faith in Christ alone and is not something they need to attain themselves (Eph 4:3). Unity is something achieved by Christ and applied by his Spirit

6 'Full text: Pope Francis' in-flight press conference from Armenia', *Catholic News Agency*, 26 June 2016 (catholicnewsagency.com/news/34103/full-text-pope-francis-in-flight-press-conference-from-armenia).
7 E.g. Wisconsin Evangelical Lutheran Synod (WELS), 'Joint Declaration on the Doctrine of Justification', WELS.net (wels.net/faq/joint-declaration-on-the-doctrine-of-justification/); see also J Bouma 'How Do Protestants and Catholics Disagree over Salvation & Justification', *Zondervan Academic*, 31 October 2016 (zondervanacademic.com/blog/how-do-catholics-and-protestants-disagree-over-salvation-justification).

when Christians from every race and tribe are brought together because of their faith in him alone.

The most important principle is that Christians *are already* united by the one Spirit, rather than *needing to appear* united with others, especially if we are not.

Holy

The breadth of use of the word 'holy' in Roman Catholicism makes a definition difficult to pin down.[8] Apart from the Holy Roman Church, there is the Holy Father, the Holy Mother of God, Holy Saints, the Holy Eucharist, and the Holy Days of Obligation (from which the English word holiday comes). There are Holy Candles, Holy Relics, the Holy Rosary and Holy Cards.

The best understanding of 'holy' for the Catholic Church is that it means to be imbued with supernatural power, uncorrupted by the natural world. In this dualistic way of thinking, holy is the opposite to natural. Because of this understanding of the word, the Catholic Church claims for itself supernatural powers that are normally only attributable to God, including:

1. infallibility—it cannot err in its *ex-cathedra* teaching[9]
2. authority—it speaks the word of God in addition to the Scriptures

---

8 Neither the Catechism of the Catholic Church (1994) or the Compendium to this catechism (2005) define 'holy'.
9 *Ex-cathedra* literally means 'from the chair'—or with the full authority of the office of the pope or bishop. A pope or bishop's statement needs to be *ex-cathedra* to be infallible in Roman Catholic teaching—i.e. a casual remark is not *ex-cathedra*.

3. power—it possesses the ability to turn bread and wine into Jesus in the Eucharistic services, and
4. eternality—the institution of the Roman Catholic Church will endure forever.

Another feature of the way 'holiness' is understood in Roman Catholicism is that it is a process that Catholics must progress through to be saved: "It is in the Church that the fullness of the means of salvation has been deposited. It is in her that by the grace of God we acquire holiness" (CCC 824). In order to be saved, Catholics need to become more holy throughout their lives, however that may be defined, but particularly by receiving the sacraments (which communicate the grace of God).

The meaning of the word 'holy' in the Greek language is about being 'set apart' or transcendent, in the sense that God and his gospel are fundamentally different to everything else in creation.[10] When 'holy' is used as a noun it is usually translated as 'saint'; as a verb, it is usually 'sanctified'; as an adjective, it is 'holy'. It is applied in the New Testament mostly to God's Spirit, the Holy Spirit. The holy church is an outworking of the activity of the Holy Spirit.

For evangelicals, a church is holy because it is a work of the Holy Spirit and is set apart from secular society for fellowship with God (Eph 1:1–14).[11] Its holiness does

---

10 The Council of Nicaea was conducted in Greek, and the New Testament and Nicene Creed were initially written in Greek before being translated into Latin.

11 In Ephesians 1:1–14, Paul writing to the saints or "holy" in Ephesus explains that they have been sealed by the Holy Spirit in order to be set apart eternally for Christ and his glory.

not come from the moral purity or performance of its members or any supernatural attributes it may claim for itself, but is solely grounded in the transcendence of God from the created world. Christians are declared holy on the basis of Christ's completed work and called to be holy as they continue to put their trust in Christ as revealed in the Scriptures (1 Cor 1:2; Eph 1:3–14). Their salvation is not dependent on their performance but on Christ's death alone.

Catholic

The original meaning of the word 'catholic' is 'according to the whole'. The Catholic Church claims that the first time the word was used to refer to the Christian church was by Ignatius of Antioch in the early second century, who said, "Wherever the bishop shall appear … there is the Catholic Church"—that is, he seemingly argued that the catholicity of the church was authorized by the bishop.[12] Catholics then move from this quote to claim that their institution is the one 'whole' or complete church, on account of its:

1. continuous succession of bishops from Peter
2. sacramental system, and
3. commitment to the ancient creeds (CCC 830).

The Roman Catholic Church considers that these three features mark out the complete or 'catholic' church in this first sense of the word.

12 Ignatius, *Epistle to the Smyrnaeans*, 8.2 (quoted in TF Torrance, *The Trinitarian Faith*, T&T Clark, 1995, p 253).

Another way the Roman Catholic Church considers itself 'catholic' is her universal mission to incorporate all people throughout the world into the Roman Catholic or 'universal' church (CCC 831). This second use of the word 'catholic' means 'universal scope'.

TF Torrance has shown that by looking to Irenaeus, who also wrote in the second century, we can see that it in fact wasn't Ignatius who first used the word 'catholic' to refer to the Christian church.[13] Rather, it was the Gnostics, and the word was used by them to ridicule Christians.

The Gnostics believed that only special religious people could have a close relationship with God. Only 'those in the know'—that's where the term 'Gnostic' comes from. Irenaeus clearly articulated the faulty thinking of the Gnostics in his work *Against Heresies* (which is one of the best surviving descriptions of Gnosticism). According to Irenaeus, Gnostics thought the idea that knowledge and relationship with God could be 'catholic', or available to all, was bizarre.

Despite the ridicule, Irenaeus fiercely defended the idea that knowledge of God is universally accessible (catholic) because Jesus, who is God, turned up in history as a human. Irenaeus argued that it is possible for *anyone* who trusts in Jesus Christ through the Scriptures to have a relationship with God—not just special people.[14] In other words, he argued that that

---

13 TF Torrance, *The Trinitarian Faith*, p 253.
14 Irenaeus, *Against Heresies*, 3.15.2 in WW Harvey (ed), Cambridge University Press, 1857.

the church is 'catholic'—universally accessible—because Jesus is fully human and fully God.[15]

Understanding the way the word 'catholic' was being used in the second century helps us to make sense of what Ignatius meant when he wrote:

> Wherever the bishop shall appear, there let the multitude [of the people] also be; even as, wherever Jesus Christ is, there is the catholic Church.[16]

Looking at Ignatius' quote in full, we can see that he is also arguing that the church is catholic (universally accessible) because of Jesus Christ: God is accessible to anyone who trusts him. Ignatius encouraged Christians to follow the leadership of a bishop, only insofar as that bishop was a reliable source of truth about Jesus, the one who is accessible to all, from the Scriptures. This was especially vital in the midst of the seemingly authoritative false teaching of the Gnostics.

The word 'catholic', when used by Rome to describe the Roman Catholic Church, means either that it is the church for the whole world (i.e. it has universal reach) or that it is the only complete or orthodox church. We can see here that Ignatius' understanding of 'catholic' contrasts with what the Roman Catholic Church teaches today.

It is sad that now the Roman Catholic Church, like the Gnostics, claims special supernatural knowledge and powers only available to itself. By doing this, it

---

15 Irenaeus, *Against Heresies*, 3.16, in Harvey (ed), 1857.
16 Ignatius, *Epistle to the Smyrnaeans*, 8.2, quoted in Torrance, *The Trinitarian Faith*, p 253.

denies the truth that all those who trust in Jesus alone through the Scriptures can have a full relationship with God. Jesus Christ is catholic, his church is catholic, his gospel is catholic—the Roman Church not so much.

Apostolic

In Greek the word 'apostle' means '*sent* one'. Jesus *sent* his followers, beginning with the Twelve, into the world:

"Therefore go and make disciples of all nations, baptizing them in the name of the Father and of the Son and of the Holy Spirit, and teaching them to obey everything I have commanded you. And surely I am with you always, to the very end of the age." (Matt 28:19–20)[17]

In the second century, Irenaeus described the apostolic foundation of the church as having a "continuously rejuvenating force".[18] This rejuvenating force was expressed as churches, enlivened by the Spirit, continued to trust in the Scriptures, written by the apostles, as their authoritative source.

When professing the apostolicity of the church today, evangelicals refer to the continued transmission of the gospel of Christ, preserved by the apostles, in the apostolic Scriptures: the New Testament. The apostolic

---

17 The word ἀποστέλλω (*apostellō*; apostle) is not used in this passage, however it is the 11 disciples (apostles) who are told to go (πορευθέντες; *poreuthentes*). This command to go does not just apply to the apostles but to all they teach, as one of the commands is for the apostles to teach "everything I have commanded you" which includes the command to go.

18 Irenaeus, *Against Heresies*, 3.38.1, in Harvey (ed), 1857.

mission continues its rejuvenating force as God's word (the Scriptures) and God's Spirit graciously prompt people to trust Christ and obey him. This is one of Christ's key teachings in his Great Commission, as he sends all Christians out to proclaim and witness to him in every nation, language and tribe throughout the world.

The Roman Catholic Church also recognizes the authority of the apostolic Scriptures and the importance of sending out Christians to hand on Jesus' teachings. But the Catholic Church teaches that in addition to the Scriptures, the traditions of the Church and the magisterium have the same authority.[19]

The Roman Catholic Church teaches that the traditions of the Church include the oral teaching of the apostles, the oral teaching of subsequent bishops whom they believe to have the same authority as the apostles (they call this apostolic succession), the teaching of past church councils, and the teaching of authorized theologians, as well as commonly accepted practices within the Roman Catholic Church.

The magisterium is the Catholic Church's official teaching authority, made up of the current pope and bishops. It claims the power of being the sole authoritative interpreter of the word of God, which includes not only the Scriptures but also all other revelations from the traditions and the magisterium.

So now, rather than there being one church united

19 *Dei verbum* 1–6. *Dei verbum* is the Second Vatican Council's 'Dogmatic Constitution on Divine Revelation' and can be viewed on the website of the Holy See (www.vatican.va/archive/hist_councils/ii_vatican_council/ documents/vat-ii_const_19651118_dei-verbum_en.html)

in faith in the one authority of Jesus Christ himself as revealed in the Scriptures, the Roman Catholic Church proclaims three expansive authorities: Scripture, the traditions of the Church and the teaching authority of the current pope and bishops.[20] This is another example of the Roman Catholic Church blurring the distinction between Christ and the Church.

Church

The word 'church' in Greek means 'gathering' or 'assembly' and is used in the New Testament to apply to religious and non-religious gatherings (Acts 19:32, 39–40). The one true church that Christians belong to (and proclaim in the creed) is the great gathering where all who have been saved by Christ are already gathered around him in worship (Heb 12:22–24). This is both a present reality in heaven and is manifest in local earthly gatherings. At these earthly gatherings, Christians worship God and build each other up in love. It is where God's people preach the word of God and administer the sacraments/ordinances of the Lord's Supper and baptism (and some would add exercising church discipline). These local gatherings are temporal, and their organisational structures, languages and cultures are varied, but nonetheless they are true and complete expressions of Christ's church.

Roman Catholics also look forward to the heavenly

---

20 Though they would argue all three reflect different facets of the one united authority that people can turn to for salvation (*Dei verbum* 10).

reality of being gathered around Christ in worship. One significant point of difference, however, is that participation in that heavenly gathering for Catholics is dependent on both Christ's atoning work on the cross as well as the co-operation of each individual Catholic with the sacramental system. Catholics may also co-operate with the sacramental system on behalf of others.

Such a system denies Catholics the assurance that they are now *already* part of the heavenly gathering and also impresses on them the burden of co-operating with the sacramental system not only for themselves but also for loved ones that may be deceased, or unable or unwilling to do so themselves.

The Roman Catholic Church defines the local church on earth structurally (CCC 832–35), as the hierarchical institution governed by the Pope and bishops and their representative priests. The most important and frequent local gathering for Catholics is the Mass, at which the sacrament of the Eucharist is conducted.

In this sacrament, members of the congregation must present bread and wine to the priest who then must consecrate it. In so doing, Catholics believe that it becomes wholly and substantially Jesus and they must worship the consecrated bread as Jesus.[21] Lay Catholics

21 The worship is directed to Christ but because of the doctrine of transubstantiation, Catholics believe Christ is wholly and substantially present in the bread and the wine once they are consecrated. In effect, the bread and wine are worshipped. For example, during the Mass's doxology, the elements are elevated and are the centre point of the liturgy. When the communicant receiving the bread and wine responds to the words, "The body/blood of Christ" with "Amen".

must take the Eucharist at least once a year, though some take it weekly.[22] Priests must celebrate the sacrament of the Eucharist daily.[23] Protestants are prohibited from receiving the Eucharist. Protestant gatherings are not considered to be particular churches but instead are referred to as lesser ecclesial communities and can only be part of the heavenly church through their association with the Roman Catholic Church.[24]

One holy catholic and apostolic church

Putting all these ideas together, we see that the one church is an expression of the unity that our one God creates through his Spirit amongst those who have faith in Christ. That church is holy because God is holy. It is set apart from this world because God and his gospel transcend this world. Yet it is also catholic—available to all—because God became human and made himself available to everyone.

The good news did not stop with Jesus' earthly ministry, because the church is also apostolic: Jesus sent out first the apostles and he continues to send out those who hear the gospel through the apostles' writings, the New Testament. These faithful men, women and children, to this day, take this good news to every people, nation, tribe and language.

22 Canon 920 of the Code of Canon Law, which can be viewed on the website of the Holy See (www.vatican.va/archive/cod-iuris-canonici/eng/documents/cic_lib2-cann208-329_en.html#TITLE_III).
23 Canon 276 of the Code of Canon Law.
24 Benedict XVI, *Mortu Proprio*, 2007. See also CCC 837–8, CCCC 168.

This gospel, through the work of the Spirit, gathers people as the church, eternally around the Father in heaven, and temporally in all sorts of different gatherings. These churches are where the true gospel is proclaimed from the Scriptures, where it is believed in and obeyed, where God is worshiped, and where his people build each-other up in love.

With the help of the Holy Spirit, the original writers of the creed—through their reflection on and application of the Scriptures—helped in articulating and clarifying such a gospel and such a church, both for believers in their time and even still for Christians today.

Questions for reflection or discussion

Read John 17.

1. How is God to be known (v 3)?

2. Unity starts with God. List all the ways that the Father and the Son are united.

3. Note all the times God's "word" is mentioned.

4. What role does God's word, spoken by Jesus and followers of Jesus, play in our unity with God and with other Christians (vv 17–23)?

9

ONE BAPTISM

Clay Kannard

We affirm one baptism for the forgiveness of sins.

Do you consider yourself a Christian? If yes, do you remember the moment you were baptized? Where did it take place? Which friends and family members were present? Was there a celebratory meal at church following the liturgy?

Perhaps you are like the many Christians who are unable to answer these kinds of questions clearly because you were baptized as a baby and all you know about your baptism is what others have told you and what you have seen in family pictures. Maybe you were even baptized more than once!

The diverse responses that can come from these kinds of questions are not insignificant when it comes to our consideration of the Nicene Creed. On the subject of baptism, the creed echoes what the apostle Paul wrote to the Ephesian church: "There is one body and one Spirit, just as you were called to one hope when you were called; one Lord, one faith, *one baptism*" (Eph 4:4–5, emphasis mine).

Jesus made it clear that baptism was integral to the work of making disciples. After his resurrection and before ascending to the right hand of God the Father, Jesus commanded his followers to go and "make disciples of all nations, *baptizing* them in the name of the Father and of the Son and of the Holy Spirit and teaching them to obey everything that I have commanded you" (Matt 28:19–20, emphasis mine).

The biblical word 'baptize' (βαπτίζειν) simply means 'to immerse' or 'to plunge'. Baptism is the initiatory ceremony in Christianity where an individual is either fully immersed in water or sprinkled with it in the name of God the Father, Son and Holy Spirit. This action signifies the individual's spiritual connection or 'union' with Jesus Christ and their participation in his death, burial and resurrection to a new life (Col 2:12). It is a public testimony of their forgiveness of sins, reception of the Holy Spirit, and inclusion into the community of Christ's followers, the universal church.

Which "one baptism" are we talking about?

Perhaps apart from the doctrine of justification, no other doctrinal theme has been as fiercely debated than the significance, means and mode of baptism. What does baptism signify? How and by whom should it be administered? What happens when a person is baptized? Is it the effective cause of their salvation? Is it *only* an outward, public testimony of their faith, or a sign and a seal of an inward change? Is baptism the basis for Christian unity?

The way we answer these questions greatly depends on our Christian tradition and understanding of baptism. Therefore, as we consider the question of whether evangelicals and Catholics can confess the Nicene Creed together, we must come to terms with the worlds behind the words, "one baptism". Are evangelicals and Roman Catholics in agreement or are we worlds apart? The scope of this chapter is not to immerse ourselves in the various views of baptism found within the evangelical faith (pun intended).[1] Rather, we will briefly examine the fundamental differences between the Roman Catholic and evangelical understandings of baptism to properly assess our creedal commitments.

Roman Catholicism's "one baptism"[2]

For Roman Catholics, the 'sacramental economy' is the way in which Christ communicates his grace to the Church through the sacraments and liturgy. The Roman Catholic Church teaches that Christ instituted the sacraments as visible signs of invisible grace, through which believers are united with God and receive spiritual

---

1   For an overview of the various theological positions for baptism within the Protestant tradition, see DG Reid's introduction in DF Wright (ed), *Baptism: Three Views*, Spectrum Multiview Books, IVP Academic, 2009.

2   For a thorough explanation of the Roman Catholic teaching on baptism and an evangelical assessment, see GR Allison, *Roman Catholic Theology and Practice: An Evangelical Assessment*, Crossway, 2014, pp 260–88.

nourishment. The sacramental economy therefore is seen as God's divine plan by which his saving work is mediated to humanity through the Church's celebration of the sacraments, and thus fostering spiritual growth and sanctification among believers (CCC 1076).[3]

As Gregg Allison highlighted in chapter 6, Roman Catholicism prioritizes baptism within its sacramental economy. Baptism is the necessary first sacrament of seven administered by the Roman Church. It is considered as the first *initiatory* sacrament for the Christian faith. The Catechism of the Catholic Church describes baptism as:

> the basis for the whole Christian life, the gateway to life in the Spirit (*vitae spiritualis ianua*), and the door which gives access to the other sacraments. Through baptism we are freed from sin and reborn as sons of God; we become members of Christ, are incorporated into the Church and made sharers in her mission: 'Baptism is the sacrament of regeneration through water in the word'. (CCC 1213)

Pope John Paul II describes baptism as "an effective sign which really purifies consciences and forgives sins".[4] In other words, Roman Catholicism teaches that the work

---

3 All references to the Catechism of the Catholic Church (CCC) can be found at www.vatican.va/archive/ENG0015/_INDEX.HTM. The number following 'CCC' refers to the paragraph being quoted.

4 John Paul II, 'General Audience: Baptism as the Foundation of Christian Life', *The Holy See*, 1 April 1998 (www.vatican.va/content/john-paul-ii/en/audiences/1998/documents/hf_jp-ii_aud_01041998.html).

of the Holy Spirit through the administered sacrament of baptism has a *causal aspect*: it *objectively effects* spiritual regeneration and opens the door to a life of faith.

'Regeneration' is the term used to describe the initial moment when God brings a person from being dead in their sin to new life in Christ. Rome views baptism as necessary for salvation, for through it the Holy Spirit is believed to purify, justify and sanctify the person (CCC 1227).[5]

When evangelicals ask their Roman Catholic friends if they have been born again, they might respond by saying, "Yes, of course! When I was baptized." This is because of what is believed to take place during the administration of the sacrament. Before a sacrament is administered, the priest will say a prayer known as *epiclesis*, asking the Holy Spirit to work through the sacrament to bring about a particular effect. For baptism, that effect is an infusion of God's grace to the individual, through the water, for their regeneration/new birth, sanctification and justification. This saving grace is received *ex opera operato*—from the work that is done. In sum, Roman Catholicism considers sacraments to be efficacious in accomplishing what they signify (*significando causant*). Pope Paul VI wrote:

> Let no one deny that *the sacraments* are acts of Christ, who administers them through the agency

5   Roman Catholic theology leaves room for those who have not received the sacrament of baptism to receive salvation (e.g. through a "baptism by blood" in the case of Christian martyrdom, or a "baptism of desire" for those who had no way to receive the sacrament but would have willingly).

of men. Therefore, *they are holy of themselves*, and owing to the virtue of Christ *they confer grace* to the soul *as they touch the body*.[6]

Roman Catholics believe baptism *causes* new life in Christ, whereas evangelicals believe this new life only to be *signified* in baptism. Rome's theology depends on human mediators using elements of nature to communicate God's grace to people.[7]

Through the mediatorial role of the priest, who is believed to represent Christ on earth and act on his behalf, water is infused with grace and effects the spiritual rebirth of the person being baptized. Through this sacrament, God's grace is 'imparted' for regeneration and new birth, the removal of original sin, the forgiveness of an individual's sins up to that point, their initial justification and sanctification, their being filled with the Holy Spirit and adopted into God's family, and the gift of faith needed to walk in this new life. All this is made possible *by the Church* and *through the work of the Church*.

It is important to note that saving faith is given *through baptism*, it does not precede baptism. Additionally, the faith received is not the faith of the individual being baptized but the faith of the community of saints,

---

6 Pope Paul VI, '*Mysterium Fidei*: Encyclical of Pope Paul VI on the Holy Eucharist', *The Holy See*, 3 September 1965 (www.vatican.va/content/paul-vi/en/encyclicals/documents/hf_p-vi_enc_03091965_mysterium.html). (Emphasis mine.)

7 This is referred to as the two 'pillars' of the Roman Catholic theological system, namely, the 'nature-grace interdependence' and the 'Christ-Church interconnection'. For an extensive explanation see chapter 2 of Allison's *Roman Catholic Theology*.

the Church. For this reason, the person being baptized, or the godparents of an infant being baptized are asked, "What do you ask of the Church?", to which they respond, "Faith!" (CCC 1253).[8] Through the sacrament of baptism, both God's regenerative work for salvation and the faith to believe in Christ are gifts given by the Church and applied through the Church's mediatorial use of water used to impart grace.

Salvation by *ex opere operato* or *sola fide*?

Since at least the time of the Protestant Reformation in the 16th century, the evangelical faith has taken issue with Roman Catholicism's sacramental understanding of salvation. The Reformation emphasized the doctrine of *sola scriptura* (Scripture alone) and the necessity of returning to the word of God as the authoritative source for knowledge of God, his plan of salvation, and how his people ought to live.

The Reformers did not discount church tradition but rather sought to ensure tradition submitted to the teaching of Scripture. As a result, the Reformers took issue with Rome's sacramental economy, its understanding of salvation by human works, and its belief in baptismal regeneration *ex opere operato* ('by the works worked').[9]

8   For this synthesis I relied on Allison's work in *Roman Catholic Theology and Practice*.
9   This refers to the Roman Catholic belief that the 'work' of the sacrament accomplishes its purpose through being administered (e.g. the act of water baptism does the work of conferring grace for the removal of original sin). It should be noted that various strands within Lutheranism share this understanding of baptismal regeneration.

Leonardo De Chirico summarizes the problem that the Reformers sought to address:

> The emphasis has shifted from the merciful God who regenerates a person out of his sovereign grace to the baptizing church that performs the sacrament of regeneration. In other words, a major shift has taken place: from the graceful act of divine salvation to the participation of the church in the saving act, and from the free gift of God to the ecclesiastical sacrament administered by the priest.[10]

Today, as the mediator and administrator of the sacraments, Rome still presumes for itself a crucial role in salvation that extends far beyond the proclamation of God's word (Rom 10:14–17). While the Catechism of the Catholic Church may state that God is not bound by the sacraments, they are certainly considered to be the normative way he conveys grace. This is especially true for baptism which is seen to cause regeneration and enable the faithful to receive God's grace through their ongoing participation in the sacramental economy.

The issue at stake is whether *salvation* (regeneration) is a result of the properly administered sacrament on an individual who might not even be able to confess faith, or if salvation is a result of God's sovereign *grace alone* (*sola gratia*) through *faith alone* (*sola fide*) in the work of *Christ alone* (*solus Christus*).

---

10 L De Chirico, *Same Words, Different Worlds: Do Roman Catholics and Evangelicals Believe the Same Gospel*, IVP, 2021, p 52.

In a paper titled 'An Evangelical Perspective on Roman Catholicism', the theological taskforce on Roman Catholicism for the World Evangelical Fellowship (now known as the World Evangelical Alliance) underlined the main issue with Rome's sacramental system. They are as follows:

- The *causal aspect* of the sacraments is in "sharp disagreement with the Scriptures".
- Their *objective efficacy* "implies an intolerable addition to the work of Christ" who has "fully accomplished the entire 'objective' side of our salvation".
- They are the "*works of human merit*, which must be mediated through the church", denying justification by faith and infringing "upon the sovereign freedom of God".[11]

After proclaiming the good news of the gospel on the day of Pentecost, the apostle Peter responded to the crowd's question about what they must do to be saved from the wrath of God. He declares: "Repent and be baptized, every one of you, in the name of Jesus Christ for the forgiveness of your sins. And you will receive the gift of the Holy Spirit" (Acts 2:38).

Luke tells us that many people who heard Peter's announcement of the gospel were cut to the heart (convicted of their sins), and that all who had received the good news that day (those who believed in the gospel proclamation) were baptized—publicly demonstrating

11 PG Schrotenboer (ed.), 'Roman Catholicism. A Contemporary Evangelical Perspective – II', *Evangelical Review of Theology*, October 1986, 10(4):87–8.

their new faith in Christ. On that day around 3,000 people were added to the church. What a scene it must have been! And in this passage, we see clearly that the people's repentance and faith preceded their baptism.

Similarly, in Acts 10 we read about the Gentiles being included in the church and we see a clear distinction between the baptism of the Spirit (regeneration) and the baptism of water: the Holy Spirit came upon the hearers of the message (v 44), *then* they were baptized (vv 47–48).

As Blocher writes, it is "the Lord who baptizes in the Spirit. His disciples baptize in water. No confusion is permitted between the two; there is no dependence of the first on the second."[12] This is a crucial distinction. As John Stott explains,

> the sacraments dramatize salvation and do not in themselves automatically convey it … It is not by the mere outward administration of water in baptism that we are cleansed and receive the Spirit, nor by the mere gift of bread and wine in Communion that we feed on Christ crucified. No, what we need is faith in the promises of God of which these things are a visible expression. What we need is faith demonstrated by our humble, believing acceptance of these signs. *But we must not confuse the signs with the promises to which*

---

12 H Blocher, 'The Nature of Biblical Unity' in JD Douglas (ed.), *Let the Earth Hear His Voice: International Congress on World Evangelization, Lausanne, Switzerland: Official Reference Volume: Papers and Reponses*, World Wide Publications, 1975, p 390.

they point. It is possible to receive the sign without receiving the promise, and also to receive the promise apart from the receiving of the sign.[13]

Scripture's assessment of Rome's "one baptism for the forgiveness of sins" is that it does indeed confuse the sign (baptism) with the promise to which it points (regeneration). Rome's theological system *requires* it to do so. The grace transmitted in the sacramental act is needed to perfect human nature, and Rome places itself at the centre of how that promise is to be received for all of humanity.

Salvation is not seen as the result of the so-called 'Great Exchange', where our sin is imputed to Christ at his death, and the perfect righteousness of Christ is freely imputed to the repentant sinner by faith (trust) alone in the gospel (2 Cor 5:21). For Rome, salvation *begins* at baptism when someone is believed to be regenerated by the Spirit through the mediation of a church that grants them faith. That faith must continuously be perfected in love through good works, especially by participating in the other six sacraments.

For evangelicals, regeneration is a result of conversion. It doesn't come from baptism, nor belonging to a certain tradition, nor by our good works, but by God's grace alone as the Holy Spirit works through the preaching of the gospel, cutting people to the heart and producing repentance and saving faith in the finished

13 J Stott, *"But I Say to You ..." Christ the Controversialist*, IVP, 2013, pp 114–5. (Emphasis mine.)

work of Christ *alone* for salvation.[14] For this reason, the Lausanne Movement's Cape Town Commitment emphasizes that baptism follows repentance and faith:

> God commands us to make known to all nations the truth of God's revelation and the gospel of God's saving grace through Jesus Christ, calling all people to repentance, faith, *baptism* and obedient discipleship.[15]

Baptism as the basis for Christian unity?

There is one additional question that must be asked when speaking of baptism. Is baptism the basis for Christian unity? Vatican II (the official teaching of Rome) and the World Council of Churches (representing many Protestant and Orthodox traditions) base Christian unity on the sign of baptism.[16] However, since the evangelical understanding does not view baptism as the sign that *precedes* faith but rather *follows* the individual's reception of faith, can baptism truly be understood as the basis of unity?

The answer is no, for as De Chirico explains, "the criterion for unity turns out to be reversed. It's not baptism that unites but it is faith received by grace alone

---

14 L De Chirico, 'To Be or Not To Be: Exercising Theological Stewardship of the Name Christian', *Foundations: An International Journal of Evangelical Theology*, Spring 2022, 82:16.

15 'The Cape Town Commitment', *Lausanne Movement*, 2010, section 10B (lausanne.org/content/ctc/ctcommitment). (Emphasis mine.)

16 *Lumen gentium* 7; cf. 'Baptism, Eucharist and Ministry (Faith and Order Paper no. 111, the "Lima Text"), *World Council of Churches*, 1982 (oikoumene.org/sites/default/files/Document/FO1982_111_en.pdf).

from God alone that unites."[17] This has been the historic position of the World Evangelical Alliance which speaks of the unity of the Spirit of "all true believers".[18]

We all know people who have been baptized yet show absolutely no signs of regeneration in their life. In the city of Rome where I live, most of the Italians I know were baptized when they were infants yet show no interest in Christ nor bear any signs of the Holy Spirit's work in their lives. Many claim the Christian identity but deny core doctrines of the faith required even by Rome.

What makes things even more confusing today is how the Roman Catholic Church now extends the basis for unity *beyond* the sacramental boundaries of baptism to a unity based on our common humanity.[19] Christian unity cannot be based on baptism alone since it is an act that bears witness to a pre-existing reality—that the baptized individual is *already* a believer. Baptism of professing believers testifies to a unity already given; it is not the basis of unity nor the guarantee that unity of faith truly exists.[20]

17 L De Chirico, 'Il battesimo e l'unità dei cristiani. Confronto con la prospettiva evangelica protestante', *Parola e Tempo* XI/11, 2012, pp 183–7. (Translation mine.)

18 'Statement of Faith', *World Evangelical Alliance* (worldea.org/who-we-are/statement-of-faith).

19 See Pope Francis, 'Encyclical Letter: *Fratelli Tutti*. Of the Holy Father Francis on Fraternity and Social Friendship', *The Holy See*, 2020 (www.vatican.va/content/francesco/en/encyclicals/documents/papa-francesco_20201003_enciclica-fratelli-tutti.html). *Fratelli tutti* ("All Brothers") is a papal encyclical that bases unity on a shared humanity, despite religious differences. This comes from Vatican II theology and is the basis for the recent developments in inter-faith prayer initiatives.

20 De Chirico, 'Il battesimo', pp 183–87.

What's at stake?

Considering the stark differences between the evangelical and Roman Catholic understanding of this section of the Nicene Creed, can we truly confess it together while maintaining our theological commitments regarding salvation? The answer to this question depends on whether we are responsible enough to look past the words being used, to the worlds that shape their understanding. When the means of salvation is at stake, evangelicals cannot afford to sacrifice God's truth at the altar of a perceived creedal unity.

> For it is by grace you have been saved, through faith—and this is not from yourselves, it is the gift of God not by works, so that no-one can boast. (Eph 2:8–9)

Questions for reflection or discussion

Read Acts 10.

1. How does God speak to Cornelius and then to Peter? What are each of their responses?

2. On whom does the Holy Spirit fall?

3. What is the place of baptism in this passage?

4. Did baptism cause Cornelius's salvation and grant him faith, or did it testify to saving faith he had already received?

10
THE WORLD TO COME
Reid Karr

*[The Son] will come again with glory
to judge the living and the dead.
His kingdom will never end.*

One day the Lord will return to reign forever—and
when he does, sin and suffering will be no more. How
wonderful will it be when death and sorrow are no
longer (Rev 21:4). This is one of the great hopes of the
Christian faith. But for this to happen, as the Nicene
Creed affirms, God will first have to judge the living
and the dead. Not everyone will enjoy eternity in the
presence of the Lord. Indeed, only those whose names
are written in the book of life will be allowed into the
presence of the Lord to enjoy his blessings for eternity
(Rev 20:11–15).

Today's Western world likes the idea of people
enjoying God's eschatological kingdom forever. It does
not like, however, God's judgement, especially if that

judgement concerns eternal punishment. That is too harsh, inhumane and unfair. The world to come must be inclusive and welcoming to all. If hell does exist, the hope is that it's empty. Indeed, the argument goes that fairness, justness and inclusiveness *demand* that hell is empty.

A careful examination of Roman Catholic theology reveals that the modern-day Catholic Church is struggling with how to answer questions about judgement and hell. This chapter will highlight how the Roman Catholic Church understands this article of the creed and will conclude with the clarity and assurance offered by God's word and the gospel of Jesus Christ.

The Roman Catholic view of the future

For this discussion it is necessary to highlight certain Roman Catholic teachings on the second coming of Christ and the coming judgement.[1] The Catholic Church teaches that all judgement has been given to the Son by the Father. His power to judge was acquired by his work on the cross. Therefore, "full right to pass definitive judgement on the works and hearts of men belongs to him as redeemer of the world" (CCC 679).[2]

After his death and resurrection, Christ ascended

1 A full description of what the Roman Catholic Church teaches on the second coming and the coming judgement can be found in the Catechism of the Catholic Church, paragraphs 668–679 and 1039–1041.

2 This book uses the standard abbreviation 'CCC' for references to the Catechism of the Catholic Church, followed by the number of the paragraph referred to. All references to the catechism can be found at www.vatican.va/archive/ENG0015/_INDEX.HTM.

into heaven. Although he was taken up and glorified after having completed his earthly mission, Christ, nevertheless, "dwells on earth in his Church" (CCC 669). There is a sense in which Christ continues his incarnation through the Church, and the Church serves as Christ's mediating agent. All judgement has been given to the Son, who continues his incarnation through the Church, which in turn mediates on the Son's behalf.[3] Although having acquired the right to judge by his work on the cross, "the Son did not come to judge but to save and to give the life he has in himself" (CCC 679). One brings judgement upon himself by rejecting grace (CCC 679).

Also relevant to this discussion is the Catholic Church's doctrine of purgatory. Those "who die in God's grace and friendship and are *perfectly* purified live for ever with Christ" in heaven (CCC 1023, emphasis mine). However, "all who die in God's grace and friendship, but still *imperfectly* purified, are indeed assured of their eternal salvation; but after death they undergo purification, so as to achieve the holiness necessary to enter the joy of heaven" (CCC 1030; emphasis mine).

Purgatory is the place where this final purification is received. Purgatory is different, however, from the

3 For a full discussion of the implications of the Catholic Church as the continuous incarnation of Christ on earth, see GR Allison, *Roman Catholic Theology and Practice: An Evangelical Assessment* (Crossway, 2014). His discussion on the 'Christ-Church interconnection' begins on page 6. See also L De Chirico, *Same Words, Different Worlds: Do Roman Catholics and Evangelicals Believe the Same Gospel?* (IVP, 2021). His discussion on this relationship begins on page 106.

punishment of the damned, who are described as those who blaspheme against the Holy Spirit. The Church's teaching on purgatory is based on the practice of praying for the dead. The Church "commends almsgiving, indulgences, and works of penance undertaken on behalf of the dead" (CCC 1032). These prayers on behalf of the dead potentially reduce the time the dead spend in purgatory and help them attain perfect purification.

In the Catechism of the Catholic Church, the Church's teaching on purgatory is immediately followed by its teaching on hell (CCC 1033–1037): "The teaching of the Church affirms the existence of hell and its eternity. Immediately after death the souls of those who die in a state of mortal sin descend into hell, where they suffer the punishments of hell, 'eternal fire'" (CCC 1035).

To bring all this together, we can see that the Church teaches that those who die and are perfectly purified go to heaven, while those who are imperfectly purified go to purgatory where they await their perfect purification. Those who die in a state of mortal sin, however, go to hell.[4] But what does all this mean for who exactly will be saved and who will face judgement?

Who will be judged?

Despite these teachings, there seems to be confusion in the Roman Catholic Church today concerning who

---

4   The catechism states that "sins are rightly evaluated according to their gravity" (CCC 1854). Sins are thus placed into one of two categories: mortal and venial sins. For an explanation and definition of these categories, see CCC 1854–1864.

exactly will be judged in the coming judgement. For example, in his 2020 encyclical *Fratelli tutti* Pope Francis claimed that we are "all brothers".[5] It is not a brotherhood forged by a common confession that Christ Jesus is Lord and our hope of salvation. Rather, it is unity based on the sharing of a common creator—a creator who is undefined.[6] Furthermore, Francis claimed that God's love is the same for everyone. This is true "regardless of religion. Even if they are atheists, his love is the same."[7]

In 2024, Pope Francis was interviewed by Fabio Fazio on the show *Che Tempo Che Fa*. Towards the conclusion of the interview Pope Francis was asked about hell. In response to Fazio's comment that it was difficult to imagine such a place, Francis agreed and stated that he would very much like to imagine that hell is empty, and that hoped he was right.[8]

He is not alone in this hope. The Catholic intellectual Richard John Neuhaus shares the same hope that

5 'Encyclical Letter: *Fratelli Tutti*. Of the Holy Father Francis on Fraternity and Social Friendship', *The Holy See*, 2020 (www.vatican.va/content/francesco/en/encyclicals/documents/papa-francesco_20201003_enciclica-fratelli-tutti.html).

6 *Fratelli tutti* concludes with two prayers: one an ecumenical Christian prayer, and the other a prayer to "the Creator", which is open to interpretation according to one's religious adherence.

7 *Fratelli tutti* 281.

8 C Wooden, 'Pope Francis says he hopes hell is "empty"', *America: The Jesuit Review*, 15 January 2024 (americamagazine.org/faith/2024/01/15/pope-francis-resign-interview-246936). The interview, which is in Italian, can be viewed here: 'Che Tempo Che Fa – Puntata 14 gennaio 2024, Inverviasta a Papa Fancesco' *Nove: Warner Bros Discovery*, January 2024 (nove.tv/che-tempo-che-fa-puntata-14-gennaio-2024-intervista-papa-francesco-video).

hell will one day be empty.[9] Placing a heavy emphasis on God's loving grace that must overcome the sin of man, the Jesuit theologian John R Sachs observes:

> It may not be said that even one person is already or will in fact be damned. All that may and must be believed is that the salvation of the world is a reality begun and established in Christ. Such a faith expresses itself most consistently in the hope that because of the gracious love of God whose power far surpasses human sin, all men and women will in fact freely and finally surrender to God in love and be saved.[10]

Prompted by Pope Francis's comments, journalist Lance Morrow recently reflected in *The Wall Street Journal* on whether hell has at this point "gone out of business".[11]

In 2018, Pope Francis made a visit to a parish church on the outskirts of Rome, where he had the opportunity to participate in a Q&A session with children of the parish. One of the children told the Pope that his father had recently died. His father did not believe in God and was an atheist but, according to the boy, was a good man and had his four children baptized. "Is my dad in heaven?" was the boy's question for Pope Francis. The

---

9 RJ Neuhaus, *Death on a Friday Afternoon: Meditations on the Last Words of Jesus from the Cross*, Basic Books, 2000, pp 42–64.

10 JR Sachs, "Current Eschatology: Universal Salvation and the Problem of Hell," *Theological Studies*, 1991, 52:252–53.

11 L Morrow, 'How We Think About Hell', *The Wall Street Journal*, 7 March 2024 (wsj.com/articles/how-we-think-about-hell-has-the-old-concept-of-fire-brimstone-gone-out-of-business-338271c7).

Pope assured the boy that his father is indeed in heaven, and that he should pray to him [12]

On what basis does Francis make this claim? On the basis of the boy's father being "a good man". Francis knew only that the boy's father was an atheist and had his children baptized. This was enough, however, to claim that he was good and that his goodness saved him.

Although the Catholic Catechism maintains the reality of judgement and hell, for Pope Francis and others, God's love, grace, compassion and mercy suggest that all will be saved in the end. His grace trumps his role as judge. In the coming judgement, the hope is that all will be saved by God's grace and be perfectly purified because, as Sachs argued above, all "will freely and finally surrender to God in love". Heaven, it is hoped, is the eschatological reality for all mankind.

The root of the confusion

Many people, including Roman Catholics, might be surprised at the Pope's suggestion that an atheist is in heaven because he was a good man, or for claiming that God's love is the same for everyone. They might be confused by his hope for an empty hell. Or perhaps the Pope's comments generate a simple, "That's just

---

12 C Wooden, '"Is my dad in heaven," little boy asks pope', *America: The Jesuit Review*, 16 April 2018, (americamagazine.org/faith/2018/04/16/my-dad-heaven-little-boy-asks-pope). The interaction between Pope Francis and the boy can be viewed here: 'Pope Francis consoles a boy who asked if his non-believing father is in Heaven', *YouTube*, 16 April 2018 (youtube.com/watch?v=bRbUTfSds0U).

Francis being Francis. He has always created doctrinal confusion. No surprise here."[13]

In any case, it is important to understand that Pope Francis, along with many Roman Catholic theologians and laypeople that share his theological convictions, have not invented anything new. Their convictions are deduced from official Roman Catholic teachings.

One such teaching is the Roman Catholic doctrine of sin. Borrowing from the teaching of Thomas Aquinas, for centuries the Catholic Church has taught that sin *wounds* human nature.[14] Think of a soldier on a battlefield who is hurt. Can he continue to contribute to the battle and advance on the enemy? That depends on the gravity of his wound. Either it causes death, at which point he is totally incapacitated and must be removed from the battlefield, or despite the wound, he is able to continue to fight and contribute to the battle, though at a reduced strength.

According to Roman Catholicism, sin does not devastate fallen man, but instead leaves his innate goodness intact. Yes, sin harms, but it does not create spiritual devastation and incapacitation. Man is still naturally good. The solider is wounded but is still able to contribute to the fight.

---

13 For more on this opinion, see Albert Mohler (host), 'Friday, March 15, 2024' [television program], *The Briefing*, 15 March 2024 (albertmohler. com/2024/03/15/briefing-3-15-24/).

14 Roman Catholicism's teaching on sin and its wound is well summarized in the CCC, paragraphs 2008–2010. For a reference to Aquinas understanding of sin as a wound to human nature, see *Summa Theologica*, first part of the second part, question 85, article 1 response.

In his 1951 encyclical *Evangelii praecones*, Pope Pius XII makes this clear when he writes: "Although, owing to Adam's fall, human nature is tainted with original sin, yet it has in itself something that is *naturally Christian* ...".[15] Post-fall man is tainted by sin, but goodness remains. He remains, in fact, naturally Christian.

The Second Vatican Council (1962–1965) would affirm and develop this concept of the naturally Christian man, indicating with greater clarity its implications. These are on full display, for example, in the Vatican II document *Lumen gentium* ('The Dogmatic Constitution on the Church'). Here the Catholic Church examines its relationship with the people who have not yet received the gospel. What is the hope and plan of salvation for them according to the Catholic Church? The Church declares that the plan of salvation:

> includes those who acknowledge the Creator. In the first place amongst these there are the Muslims, who, professing to hold the faith of Abraham, along with us adore the one and merciful God, who on the last day will judge mankind. Nor is God far distant from those who in shadows and images seek the unknown God, for it is He who gives to all men life and breath and all things, and as Saviour wills that all men be saved. Those also can attain to salvation who through no fault of their own do not know the Gospel of

15 *Evangelii praecones* 57 (www.vatican.va/content/pius-xii/en/encyclicals/documents/hf_p-xii_enc_02061951_evangelii-praecones.html). (Emphasis mine.)

Christ or His Church, yet sincerely seek God and moved by grace strive by their deeds to do His will as it is known to them through the dictates of conscience. Nor does Divine Providence deny the helps necessary for salvation to those who, without blame on their part, have not yet arrived at an explicit knowledge of God and with His grace strive to live a good life. Whatever good or truth is found amongst them is looked upon by the Church as a preparation for the Gospel.[16]

Although this text contains many nuances and is interpreted differently even in Catholic circles, we can nonetheless see why Pope Francis confidently claims that we are "all brothers". It is difficult to say otherwise in light of *Lumen gentium.* If Muslims are our brothers, and if those who don't know the gospel but strive to live good lives are all included in the plan of salvation, it would seem that with few exceptions, we are indeed all brothers.

This affirms that although humanity has been tainted and wounded by sin, we are nonetheless naturally Christian. *Lumen gentium* speaks of the last day when mankind will be judged, but it creates confusion regarding who will be judged and who will not attain perfect purification, thus giving credence to Francis's hope that hell will be empty.

---

16 *Lumen   gentium*   16   (www.vatican.va/archive/hist_councils/ii_vatican_council/documents/vat-ii_const_19641121_lumen-gentium_en.html).

Evangelical and Catholic agreement

What does all this mean for evangelical and Catholic agreement concerning the coming judgement and a shared confession of this declaration of the Nicene Creed?

For the evangelical, the answering begins with an examination of what God's word says on the matter, starting with what it says about fallen humanity. Is it right to say, as the Catholic Church teaches, that while sin has wounded our nature, it nonetheless remains naturally Christian?

With clarity Paul writes to the Ephesians that we are *dead* in our sins and trespasses and are by nature "children of wrath" (Eph 2:1–3, ESV). To the Corinthians, Paul says that for "the natural person" the things of the Spirit—that is, the things of God which are revealed through the Spirit—are folly to him, and he is unable to understand and interpret them (1 Cor 2:14, ESV). This is a far cry from a mere wound and the understanding of the 'natural Christian'. If we are dead in our sin, as God's word says, there is no life in us whatsoever. Until new life is miraculously breathed into us, we remain dead, unable to make any movement towards God.

While hell is a place that does exist according to Roman Catholicism, Roman Catholic theology, and especially Vatican II theology, has blurred its teaching on the coming judgement. It is unclear on who indeed will die in a state of mortal sin and go to hell. Instead, Roman Catholic theology legitimizes Pope Francis's hope that when the Son comes in glory to judge the living and the dead, all will be welcomed into his presence and receive eternal life. This is because we are all brothers, all naturally Christian, and all included in the plan of salvation.

Concerning the coming judgement, however, the Bible does not permit ambiguity and confusion. The Son will indeed judge the living and the dead (John 5:25–29; 2 Tim 4:1; Rom 14:10; 2 Cor 5:10), and it is clear who will receive eternal reward, and who will receive eternal punishment. Eternal life is secured in the completed work of Jesus Christ on the cross and in his resurrection. Christ is the sinner's hope because even though Jesus knew no sin, in obedience to the Father he became sin, so that whoever believes in him might "become the righteousness of God" and be justified before the Father (2 Cor 5:21).

We are all sinners and stand condemned before the Lord, destined for eternal judgement. But praise be to God, for we can be justified by his grace as a gift through the redemption that is in Jesus Christ. This redemption is received through faith, so that in Christ there is now no condemnation for the sinner (Rom 3:23–25, 8:1).

Thanks to this doctrine of justification, the doctrine of purgatory is rendered useless. Through justification we are declared righteous and are perfectly purified by the blood of Christ (Rom 5:1, 9; Heb 9:14; 1 John 1:7). There is no need for a time of purification or for the prayers of others on our behalf, for we are purified in and through Christ. For this reason, "salvation is found in no-one else, for there is no other name under heaven given to mankind by which we must be saved" (Acts 4:12).

In his state of sin man can make no movement towards God. In his own strength he cannot ascend to heaven. He cannot even make the first step, for due to his sin he lies dead on the battlefield. His only hope is in the Father who graciously descends to him in the incarnate Son and in the power of the Holy Spirit, bringing new life to where there was previously death (2 Cor 5:17; Ezek 37:5–6). John Calvin describes this beautifully when he writes:

> By his own descent to earth he has prepared our ascent to heaven. Having received our mortality, he has given us his immortality. Having undertaken our weakness, he has made us strong in his strength. Having taken upon himself the burden of unrighteousness with which we were oppressed, he has clothed us with his righteousness ... This is the wondrous exchange made by his boundless goodness.[17]

This "wondrous exchange" is sinful man's great eschatological hope. With it he can face the coming judgement with the assurance of who the Father declares him to be in Christ Jesus through the power of the Holy Spirit.

Evangelicals and Catholics affirm the same words of the Nicene Creed, but they confess different worlds and realities theologically speaking, and these different realities undermine the ability to truly confess the creed together.[18]

---

17 Calvin, *Institutes of the Christian Religion*, 4.17.2, trans. H Beveridge, Christian Classics Ethereal Library (ccel.org/ccel/calvin/institutes. vi.xviii.html).

18 For a thorough discussion of the reality of Catholics and evangelicals having many words in common, with those words representing different theological realities, see De Chirico's aforementioned *Same Words, Different Worlds*.

Questions for reflection or discussion

Read Ephesians 2:1–10.

1. What are the implications of being dead in our sin?

2. How does God make us alive in Christ?

3. What is the role of good works in our salvation?

4. Why is the Roman Catholic doctrine of purgatory contrary to evangelical theology?

11

IS NICAEA ENOUGH?

Bradley G. Green

Throughout their history, Christians have determined it necessary to articulate the faith. Whether we call these articulations 'creeds', 'confessions' or 'statements' is somewhat beside the point as every effort of this sort shares a basic family resemblance: the desire to articulate something important, essential or pressing about what we believe. Some Protestants use various creeds, confessions and statements more than others, but all have generally affirmed the importance of such documents.

The purpose of this concluding chapter is to ask a basic question: is Nicaea enough? Or, more specifically: is the Nicene Creed (381 AD) adequate as a summary of Christian belief, confession, fellowship and shared ministry? The more one reflects on this question, the more one sees what a complex question it is.

If one is asking whether all Christians should affirm

the Nicene Creed, the answer should be a hearty 'yes'.[1] But if one comes from a different angle and asks the more complex question (of whether the Nicene Creed is optimal or sufficient or enough for meaningful Christian belief, confession, fellowship and shared ministry) then a different answer might emerge. In short, if one asks the latter kind of question, I want to suggest that the Nicene Creed is *not* enough. It is this second question we will focus on in this chapter.

Why the desire to see the Nicene Creed as enough?

We might begin by asking *why* would one be inclined to think that Nicaea might be enough for Christian belief, confession, fellowship and shared ministry? One reason might be the understandable impulse or desire for unity. There is a right and proper yearning, on my view, for Christian unity. Most of us would not—generally—seek to live a life of tension, friction, disharmony and disagreement. If we are honest, most of us probably think along the following lines: "It would be nice to live a life where we get along with all or most people, and where our lives are not marked by combat, fighting, debating and constant disagreement".

---

1   Though Calvin's reservations about the exact way to understand the source of the Son's deity is a legitimate reservation with which I have sympathy. Calvin speaks to this in his *Expositio impietatis Valentini Gentilis*, found in G Baum, E Cunitz and E Reiss (eds), *Opera quae supersunt omnia*, vol 9, p 369 in *Calvini Opera* (vol 37 of *Corpus Reformatorum*, Brunswick, 1970). Robert Letham has a helpful summary in his book, *The Holy Trinity: In Scripture, Theology, and Worship*, P&R, 2004, pp 261–263.

We know from Scripture that a day *is* coming where there will be a blessed and joyous unity. Indeed, we know that in the future the wolf will lie down with lamb (Isa 11:6). But we also know that it is a mark of unfaithfulness and unbelief to say, "peace, peace" when there is no peace (Jer 8:11; Ezek 13:10).

But it is a mistake—a serious one—to yearn in the wrong way, or to yearn for unity without grasping *where* one is in history. Political commentator and theorist Eric Voegelin warned against "immanentizing the eschaton".[2] By this terminology, Voegelin meant that it is a perennial temptation to try to coerce the blessed future eschatological state into the present by the use of force (Voegelin was particularly concerned about what happens when centralized political power attempts to 'usher' in the eschaton, as had happened in the 20th century).

Perhaps it is also mistaken to so wish for peace and unity, that one fails to have the courage to live in our age of antithesis, where there is a fundamental hostility between the things of the evil one and the things of God (Gen 3:15). That is, we live in a period of spiritual battle. The future state of unity and peace has not fully arrived.

It is wise and faithful to know our place in God's economy. Thus, we should both (1) seek unity where we can, but we should also (2) know that we shall not find perfect unity in the present time. This sought-after

2   One can find this theme in Eric Voegelin's magisterial five-volume *Order and History* (first published with Louisiana State University Press from 1956 through 1987) or Voegelin's own summary of his thought in the much shorter, *New Science of Politics* (University of Chicago Press, 1952).

unity, of course, is a unity sought by and among professing Christians.

The belief that the Nicene Creed is enough for unity is perhaps rooted in a desire to return to an age where the universal church seemed—at least in broad outline—to be a united church with a common theology. But this was only somewhat the case historically. In the fourth century, Nicene trinitarianism 'won' in 325 AD at Nicaea (and again in 381 AD at Constantinople). But Athanasius, the leading proponent of Nicene trinitarianism in the fourth century, was banished from his position as bishop some five times over 17 years during his ministry. In short: the church was only ever united to a certain degree.

Or perhaps the belief that the Nicene Creed is sufficient stems from the conviction that once one has got the Trinity and the deity of the Son and Spirit figured out, that is enough. That is, can't the church simply rally around a simple confession that there is one God, and that the Father, Son and Holy Spirit are each fully divine persons?

Certainly, a Christian should confess no *less* than this, but is there any good reason to think that such a confession is *enough*? As we shall suggest below, to somehow see the doctrine of God or a high view of Christ and the Holy Spirit as enough leaves us in an awkward and untenable situation when we try to articulate the importance of things like grace and justification by faith alone. Many of these issues are dealt with in earlier chapters of this book.

John Henry Newman and James Orr

We might find help in the 1901 work *The Progress of Dogma*, by Scottish divine James Orr.[3] Orr was one of the leading Protestant theologians of his era. But to understand his work, we must briefly recall the work of John Henry Newman. Orr wrote his volume just over ten years after the death of Newman (1801–1890). Newman was a prominent thinker during his era and has had significant impact on (especially) Roman Catholic thought since his time. He converted from Calvinism to Anglo-Catholicism, and eventually to Roman Catholicism. Among other contributions, he is known for a creative way of thinking about the development of doctrine over time (see Newman's *An Essay on the Development of Doctrine*).[4]

Rome, in general and until the time of Newman, tended to want to say that the Roman Catholic dogmatic system could more or less be found in the earliest days of the church. Newman offered a different understanding, which has alleviated Rome of the burden of having to find its theology in the earliest history of the church.

In short, Newman argued that the development of doctrine can be thought of as analogous to how a seed grows into a tree. Over time, the tree grows, certain parts are pruned, and other parts are encouraged in

---

3   J Orr, *The Progress of Dogma*, James Clark and Co., 2002 (originally published in 1901).

4   JH Newman, *An Essay on the Development of Christian Doctrine*, University of Notre Dame Press, 1994 (a reprinting of the 1878 version).

their growth. It might seem difficult to recognize that the present tree comes from such a small seed, but if you could go back and observe, one would be able to discern a real, organic connection between the seed and the full-grown tree.

Partially in response to Newman, James Orr offered his own understanding of how doctrine (or dogma) grows or changes over time. Orr differed from Newman in that Orr—as a Protestant—did not feel the theological pressure to organically link all later official Catholic teaching to the earliest Christian movement (the New Testament). Yet Orr seemed to sense a need to help Protestants think about how the church can grow and develop in its theological understanding *without* having to bear the burden of somehow justifying every doctrinal affirmation that the church has made throughout its history.

Orr creatively suggested that the church—as we look back through time—*has* tended to work through a certain doctrine for one era, then another doctrine in the following era, and so on. That is, there is only so much time and mental energy to work on a particular doctrine at a given time.

So, in the first and second centuries, the church seemed to focus on working out its understanding of religious authority, seen in the forming of the New Testament canon. Then, in the third and fourth centuries, the church devoted itself to working out key elements of the doctrine of the Trinity (especially the Son's relationship to the Father, and then the person of the Holy Spirit). Then, in the fourth and fifth centuries the church devoted itself to working through the person of Christ (culminating in Chalcedon in 451 AD), as well as working through the doctrine of God's grace (as seen in the debates between Augustine and the Augustinians against Pelagius and the Pelagians).

Orr's work may not be the final word on the matter, but it provides one way of thinking through how and why the church has seemed to focus on certain doctrines at certain points in its development. Nick Needham has suggested that Orr may have been unduly influenced by a too-optimistic view of the church's growth and progress throughout history.[5] Nevertheless, Orr can help evangelicals to think through how it is perfectly reasonable for the church to improve or develop in its doctrinal understanding over time. And Orr shows us that we need not see the Nicene Creed as the high point of doctrinal development. Rather, we might *expect* to see the church grow in the way it understands and articulates Christian truth after that point.

The development of doctrine and creeds

Orr is helpful in encouraging us to look for *further* and *necessary* creedal and doctrinal development over time. But perhaps a more biblical perspective on the development of doctrine would say something like the following: the church *does* continue to develop its doctrine as it mines the Scriptures—we should anticipate

5   N Needham, 'The Tragic Enigma of John Henry Newman', *CRN Journal*, Spring 2001, p 15.

that God will continue to break forth fresh things from his word by the Spirit, even as conflicts, challenges and heresies are encountered.

But we need not see the church's growth in doctrinal understanding as a linear process. Instead, the church's development of its doctrinal creeds and understandings are likely much more like a jagged line on a chart than the kind of positive trend line that someone might want to see in the returns on their financial investments.

Let's think of the history of Israel. In the history of Israel, we see *success* at times and serious *failure* at other times. In 1 Kings 3–10 we see significant success in Israel under Solomon's wise leadership. We witness Solomon's wisdom, the growth of Solomon's kingdom, Solomon's building of the temple, the Queen of Sheba's visit to Solomon, and the recounting of Solomon's wealth at the end of chapter 10. But then 1 Kings 11 begins with recounting Solomon's fall, and we read that "the LORD became angry with Solomon because his heart had turned away from the LORD" (v 9).

We know that eventually Israel falls to Assyria in 722 BC, and that Judah falls to Babylon in 586 BC. In short, we see blessed success and tragic failure—at times in the very same narratives. This same kind of jagged history of success and failure is something we might expect to see in the *rest* of history.

All Christians have, ultimately, an 'optimistic' eschatology. We know that one day, the earth will be full of the knowledge and the glory of the Lord "as the waters cover the sea" (Isa 11:9; Hab 2:14). We may disagree about the details, but all Christians know—at least in the broad contours—how this story ends. God wins. But between now and the end of all things we are certainly *not* promised a smooth journey to the ultimately victorious ending of all things.

Thus, in church history we should expect and anticipate God's ultimate victory over all evil. But we should also anticipate that the path from our present to the ultimate end will likely be rocky—full of beautiful doctrinal understandings and affirmations, but also full of bizarre and perverse doctrinal collapse and heresies. For this reason, we should anticipate and labour towards continual and repeated efforts to articulate the Christian faith as clearly and persuasively as we can.

Let's look now at two crucial and beautiful developments in doctrine that occurred after the time of Nicaea, which show the limits of the creed as the basis of Christian confession.

Augustine (AD 354–430) and the grace of God

First, Augustine's articulation of the grace of God in salvation would seem to be—to many of us—a proper working out of implicit and explicit biblical truths. Augustine's theology of grace was worked out in the late fourth and early fifth centuries in response to Pelagius and the Pelagians.[6]

---

6 In brief, Pelagianism denied that post-fall man comes into the world as sinful. Post-fall man can indeed keep all of God's moral commands apart from any sort of efficacious grace. I have dealt with the protracted debate between Augustine and Pelagius/the Pelagians in my book, *Augustine of Hippo: His life and impact*, Christian Focus, 2020, pp 70–85.

This prompts us to ask: should at least *some* meaningful understanding of God's grace be a part of a basic confession of faith? Should Pelagianism be considered within the bounds of Christian orthodoxy?

A good case can be made that Augustine's articulation of grace is an insightful articulation of what is in the Bible. As such, a confession of the grace of God should be found in any statement or creed that serves as a good summary of Christian belief. Yet this is something that was not articulated at Nicaea.

The Reformation and justification by faith alone

Second, the doctrine of justification by faith alone, as articulated during the time of the Protestant Reformation, occurs *well* past the time of Nicaea—by some 1200 years. Protestants have historically believed that the Reformers were not first and foremost *innovators* (as Jacopo Sadoleto labelled the Protestants in his 1539 letter to the Genevans). Rather, Protestants have historically believed that the Reformers were *recovering a fundamentally biblical insight*: namely, that sinners are declared righteous by God (the one who justifies), on the basis of Christ's finished work (the ground of justification), and through the instrument of faith alone (the means of justification).

The Reformers simultaneously *recovered* a biblical insight and *sharpened* a key biblical insight in the midst of conflict and debate. The Reformation's recovery of the doctrine of justification by faith alone is either a good and right expression of Christian truth, or it is a real mistake.

Protestants continue to rightly believe that the New Testament doctrine of justification became muddled and confused over time, and that in response to this, the Reformation was a helpful recovery of the truth, and not a departure from apostolic Christianity. No appeal to the Nicene Creed will settle that question, as important and wonderful as the Nicene Creed is. We can therefore see another limitation of the creed as the basis of shared Christian unity.

Looking backward and forward

Christians can look back with awe and gratitude at how God has led Christians to articulate and clarify the faith throughout its history. Christians can simultaneously affirm *past* creedal wisdom like that of the Nicene Creed, as well as gratefully recognize that God has *continued* to lead his church into truth and wisdom since then—not least with Augustine's articulation of grace and the Reformation's recovery of justification by faith alone. The biblical Christian will be simultaneously looking backward and forward. The biblical Christian will give thanks for *past* wisdom and will be looking *forward* to what is required in his or her own day.

There is no good reason to somehow assert that the church's doctrinal development in the fourth century can never be re-thought, or fine-tuned, or sharpened. Rather, God's church grows and develops its doctrinal understanding over time. One need not follow John Henry Newman and see an organic development from the 'seed' of earliest Christianity to the current Roman

Catholic Church. And one need not even follow James Orr's understanding of 'the progress of dogma'—though his construal has its strengths. Rather, we should expect that God would continue to lead his people over time, and that as God's Spirit works in God's people, they continue to develop and fine-tune the church's doctrinal understanding.

We should also expect that the church will *grow* in its understanding over time, almost certainly necessitating the repeated articulation and explanation of its doctrinal beliefs. We should also not be surprised if God, in his grace, leads the church to express its understanding of Christian truth with increasing clarity. And we should not be surprised if at times, under God's gracious hand, the church recovers certain truths that have become somewhat confused or muddled or even lost over the centuries. And neither should we be surprised if God, in his mercy, allows Christians to sharpen truths, and even draw out new and wondrous things from our old, old canon.

For now, we can and *should* joyfully proclaim the truths found in the Nicene Creed while recognizing its limits as a basis for meaningful Christian belief, confession, fellowship and shared ministry. This book has shown at each turn that the creed is not enough as a foundation of unity between evangelicals and Catholics. While evangelicals may speak the same creed as our Roman Catholic friends, we have seen that we possibly understand the beautiful words contained therein from different angles, which leads to different implications in our respective theological systems.

Questions for reflection or discussion

Read Ephesians 1:3–14.

1. List the doctrines the Nicene Creed and this passage *both* state. (A doctrine is the teachings from the Bible on a specific topic.)

2. List the doctrines that this passage from Ephesians includes that are *absent* in the Nicene Creed.

3. At the time of the Reformation, the question, "Can Christians have assurance of salvation?" became an important question for churches to answer. How helpful are each of the doctrinal statements that you have listed in answering this question?

4. What is a doctrinal question you find Christians commonly struggle with today? Where in the Bible would you go for answers?

GLOSSARY

Anthropology: The study of humans.

Apparition: An unexpected appearance.

Aquinas, Thomas: A 13th-century Italian theologian regarded by the Roman Catholic Church as their most important theologian.

Arianism: A heresy that insisted that Jesus was not the eternal Son of God, but rather a created being.

Assumption of Mary (The): A dogma or teaching of the Roman Catholic Church, proclaimed by Pope Pius XII in 1950, claiming that Mary was assumed into heaven body and soul without her body experiencing decay.

Athanasius: Bishop of Alexandria in 328 AD. A strong defender of the doctrine of the incarnation of Jesus Christ.

Atonement: A term referring to the way that Jesus' death pays for our sins.

Augustine: A highly regarded fifth-century theologian and North African bishop who argued, against Pelagius, that humans receive salvation as a gift, not as a reward for choosing God.

Beatific vision: An aspect of theology that focuses on the effect of seeing God.

Begotten: Fathered by.

Calvin, John: A key early Reformer of the church in the 16th century, based in Continental Europe.

Canon: The books of the Old and New Testaments; the completed Bible.

Capax Dei: Literally 'capable of God' or naturally oriented towards God.

Cape Town Commitment, The: A statement of shared biblical convictions issued from a meeting in South Africa in 2010 where more than 4,000 Christian leaders gathered from 198 countries.

Cappadocian Fathers: Three theologians born shortly after the Council of Nicaea in 325 AD: Basil of Caesarea; Basil's younger brother Gregory, who was later Bishop of Nyssa and so known as Gregory of Nyssa, and Gregory of Nazianzus. They are especially known for their trinitarian theology.

Catechism of the Catholic Church (CCC): A document produced by the Catholic Church under Pope John Paul II in 1992. Available in English at the website of the Holy See (www.vatican.va/archive/ENG0015/_INDEX.HTM). It was added to by Pope Benedict in 2006 with the Compendium to the Catechism of the Catholic Church (CCCC), which is a more concise version written in a question and answer format also available in English at *The Holy See* website (www.vatican.va/archive/compendium_ccc/documents/archive_2005_compendium-ccc_en.html).

Christ-Church interconnection: A term coined by Gregg Allison in his book *Roman Catholic Theology and Practice: An Evangelical Assessment* to describe the Roman Catholic teaching that the Catholic Church is a continuation of the presence of Jesus in the world, assuming some of his divine attributes.

Consecration: The process of setting something or someone apart for a special religious purpose.

Constantine I: A fourth-century Roman emperor who converted to Christianity. He legalized the practice of Christianity and wanted the church to become an ally of the empire.

Consubstantial: Of the same substance.

Coram Deo: Literally, 'in God's presence'.

Council of Chalcedon: A council of church leaders in 451 AD. The council articulated that the two natures of Christ (divine and human) are without confusion, without change, without division and without separation.

Council of Constantinople (First): A council of church leaders in 381 AD where the divinity of the Holy Spirit was clearly affirmed.

Council of Ephesus: A council of church leaders in 431 AD where Mary was given the title "Mother of God".

Council of Nicaea (First): A council of church leaders in 325 AD where Jesus was affirmed as being fully God and fully man.

Docetism: A heretical belief system that claimed Jesus only appeared to be a human being.

Doctrine: Christian teaching.

Ecclesiology: The doctrine of the church.

Eschatology: The doctrine of the end times.

Eschatological: Relating to the doctrine of the end times.

Evangelical: A worldwide, interdenominational Christian movement that places the *evangel*, or gospel, at the centre of Christian belief. This gospel is that Jesus, fully human and fully God, died to pay for our sins completely and rose bodily from the dead to assure our eternal relationship with the Father if we put our trust in him. The other key aspect of evangelical belief is that the 66 books of the Bible are the only ultimate authority for Christian teaching.

Ex opera operato: Literally 'from the work that is done'. When referring to the Roman Catholic sacrament of baptism, it means that the action of baptism brings about regeneration.

Faith: Trust, dependence, reliance. Occasionally used as a noun to refer to a body of teaching—i.e. "the faith" (Jude 1.3).

Gentile: Anyone who doesn't have a Jewish background.

Gnosticism: A Greek philosophical movement that claimed certain special people could attain special knowledge (or 'gnosis'), especially of God or the gods.

Godhead: A way of describing the three-person nature of the one God.

Grace: A free, unmerited gift of God, most commonly applied to the gift of being saved from the punishment our sins deserve.

Homoiousios: Of a similar substance.

Homoousios: Of the same substance. Note the important difference between '*homoousios*' and '*homoiousious*'.

Ignatius of Antioch: A disciple of the apostle John writing in the first and early-second centuries. A leader in Antioch in Syria and key authority on Christian theology.

Imago Dei: In the image of God.

Immaculate conception of Mary: A false dogma or teaching of the Roman Catholic Church, proclaimed by Pope Pius IX in 1854, claiming that Mary the mother of Jesus was conceived by her parents without any stain of sin.

Imparted: Placed on another.

Imputed: Counted to another.

Incarnation: The Son of God becoming human in Jesus.

Infallible: Incapable of error.

Irenaeus: A key Christian leader, writer and theologian from Lyon in France in the second century.

Justification (the doctrine of): A key issue in the Protestant Reformation. Simply put, the belief that people are declared right with God (justified) by the work of God alone in Christ through his death on the cross. People receive this as a gift by trusting Christ—that is, through faith alone. In contrast, the Roman Catholic Church teaches that justification requires ongoing cooperation with the Roman Catholic sacramental system.

Lumen gentium: Literally 'a light to the nations'. A document from the Second Vatican Council of the Roman Catholic Church (Vatican II) written in 1964, focusing on the Roman Catholic Church's relationship with non-Roman Catholic religions and beliefs.

Luther, Martin: A monk and Bible translator whose critique of the Christian Church (the 95 Theses) in 1517 is considered to be the trigger for the Reformation.

Magisterium, The: The teaching office of the Roman Catholic Church formed by the pope, cardinals and bishops which, according to the Catholic Church, has authority to interpret and proclaim the word of God for the world. This word of God includes but is not restricted to the Bible.

Mariology: A branch of study that focuses on Mary, Jesus' mother, as its subject.

Mass: The name for the Roman Catholic church service where they teach that bread and wine are consecrated and, through the work of the Holy Spirit, become wholly Jesus Christ in the sacrament of the Eucharist (this occurs by a process known as transubstantiation). Priests are obliged to conduct this service daily. All Catholics are encouraged to attend a service at least weekly.

Mortal sin: In Roman Catholicism, a serious breaking of God's law that is done with full knowledge and complete consent. Dying with a mortal sin that has not been forgiven precludes someone from entering heaven.

Nature-grace interdependence: A term coined by Gregg Allison in his book *Roman Catholic Theology and Practice* to describe a key aspect of Roman Catholic teaching which asserts that after the fall, the created world retains a natural capacity to receive and transmit divine attributes. This is done particularly through the sacramental system. The realm of grace, or the supernatural realm, needs the created realm to be able to transmit divine attributes.

Newman, John Henry: A 19th-century theologian who moved from evangelicalism to Anglo-Catholicism, then to Roman Catholicism and became a Roman Catholic cardinal and then saint.

Ordinances: A way of describing ceremonies ordered by Jesus, namely baptism and the Lord's Supper.

Original sin: In Roman Catholicism, the teaching that all humans (apart from Mary and Jesus) are born with a macula or spot inherited from Adam. This spot impairs some human attributes. It is removed by the infusion of grace in the sacrament of baptism. In contrast, the Protestant teaching on total depravity teaches that all human attributes have been corrupted by sin such that humans are slaves to sin. The only remedy for this is by the unilateral work of God in Jesus, received by faith, resulting in a spiritual rebirth and an assurance of ongoing forgiveness and an eternal relationship with God.

Orthodox churches: A branch of Eastern Christian churches that separated from the Western churches centred around Rome in 1050 AD.

Orthodoxy: Commonly held and consistent teaching.

Pelagius: A fifth-century British monk who is known for teaching that humans are innately good and therefore can and must choose God, and that they receive salvation as a reward for that choice.

Penal substitution: The teaching that Jesus by his death paid the complete penalty for the sins of those who put their faith or trust in him on their behalf.

Penance: According to the Roman Catholic Church, actions that are required for a person to contribute to the payment of the debt to God their sin incurs.

Perpetual virginity of Mary: The belief that Mary remained a virgin throughout her life.

Postlapsarian: Referring to after the fall of Adam and Eve.

Preposition: A word that relates elements of a sentence to each other, usually describing time, direction, place or relationship.

Purgatory: In Roman Catholic thought, a place—

physical or spiritual—where unpaid debts to God are paid by suffering before a person can go to heaven.

Reformation, The: A period of intense review and change in the teachings and practices of the Christian church in Continental Europe, Ireland and the United Kingdom during the 16th and 17th centuries.

Regeneration: The moment a person is spiritually reborn, moving from being spiritually dead to alive.

Rosary: A tactile form of prayer, principally to Mary, usually involving a strand of beads to help count the number of prayers made. The prayers that compose the Rosary are arranged in 'decades' or sets of ten 'Hail Marys', a prayer of veneration to Mary. Each 'decade' is preceded by one 'Our Father' (the Lord's Prayer) and followed by the 'Glory Be' ("Glory be to the Father and to the Son and to the Holy Spirit, as it was in the beginning, is now and ever shall be, world without end"). The Rosary concludes with the 'Hail Holy Queen', another prayer of veneration to Mary.

Sacramental economy: The Roman Catholic sacramental system, which is the way the Catholic Church believes that God communicates his benefits in the created world.

Sadoleto, Jacopo: A 16th-century cardinal in Geneva, known for his criticism of Calvin's teaching on justification by faith alone.

Salvation history: The time in human history from the creation of the world till the return of Christ.

Second Vatican Council: See 'Vatican II'.

Sola fide: Literally 'faith alone' (or 'trust alone').

Sola scriptura: Literally 'Scripture alone', indicating that the Bible is the final or ultimate authority for knowledge of God.

Soteriological: Referring to the doctrine of salvation.

Syncretism: The capacity of a religious system to absorb the teaching and practices of other religious systems.

Theotokos: Literally 'God bearer'. A term attributed to Mary, the mother of Jesus, at the Council of Ephesus in 431 AD to reinforce the teaching that Jesus was fully human and fully God.

Transcendence: A characteristic of God referring to him being beyond and greater than anything in the created world.

Trinitarian: Relating to the doctrine of the Trinity—the belief that one God exists as three persons: Father, Son and Spirit.

Vatican II: An abbreviation of the Second Vatican Council, a council held by leaders of the Roman Catholic Church from 1962–1965.

Veneration: A form of spiritual devotion that approaches worship. Includes praying to and through a deceased person, their image, or a relic from their life. Angels can be venerated as well as humans. It is distinguished in Roman Catholic theology from *latria*, which is another form of worship only appropriate for God.

CONTRIBUTORS

Gregg R. Allison is professor of Christian theology at the Southern Baptist Theological Seminary. Gregg received his PhD at Trinity Evangelical Divinity School. He is secretary of the Evangelical Theological Society and a book review editor for the *Journal of the Evangelical Theological Society*. He is the author of numerous books, including *Roman Catholic Theology and Practice: An Evangelical Assessment* (2014), *Historical Theology: An Introduction to Christian Doctrine* (2011), *Embodied* (2021) and *40 Questions about Roman Catholicism* (2021).

Robbie Bellis is a pastor of the Eglise Protestante Evangélique of Louvain-la-Neuve, a church he helped plant in 2020 in a university town in French-speaking Belgium. He obtained his ThM from Westminster Seminary Philadelphia. His thesis was on the decline of the belief of penal substitution in the Roman Catholic Church during the 20th century. Robbie also lectures at the Institut Biblique de Bruxelles, which is helping to train future pastors and church workers in Belgium. He is married and has four children.

Rachel Ciano lectures in Christianity in History at Sydney Missionary and Bible College, Australia. With her husband, she has ministered in Australia and the UK. In 2009, they planted a church in a multicultural area of Sydney which is one-third Catholic, and they continue to serve and lead there. She is co-author of *10 Dead Guys You Should Know* (2021), and the apt sequel, *10 Dead Gals You Should Know* (2023).

Leonardo De Chirico is the pastor of Breccia di Roma. His PhD is from King's College London; it was published as *Evangelical Theological Perspectives on Post-Vatican II Roman Catholicism* (2003). He has written multiple other works, including *Same Words, Different Worlds: Do evangelicals and Roman Catholics believe the same gospel?* (2021) and *Engaging with Thomas Aquinas: An Evangelical Approach* (2024). He is a lecturer of Historical Theology at Istituto di Formazione Evangelica e Documentazione in Padova, Italy, and Director of the Reformanda Initiative/RSLN.

Alastair Dunlop has been the pastor of Howth and Malahide Presbyterian Church in Dublin since 2013 (the church is part of the Presbyterian Church in Ireland and is affiliated with the Dublin Gospel Partnership). He previously served in pastoral ministry in Northern Ireland, which is where he grew up. He is married with three young children and loves rugby.

Mark Gilbert works for Certainty4Eternity, an organization established to help churches share the gospel with people from a Roman Catholic background. He currently works as a chaplain on the Northern Beaches of Sydney. Mark has published a number of resources to help people share the good news about Jesus with people from a Roman Catholic background including *The God Who Saves* (2006), *The Road Once Travelled* (2010) and *Stepping Out in Faith* (2012).

Bradley G. Green is a professor of Systematic Theology at Union University (Jackson, Tennessee) where he serves on the Board of Directors at the Augustine School. Brad received his ThM from Southwestern Baptist Theological Seminary and his PhD from Baylor University. He is a member of the Board of Directors of American Friends of Tyndale House Cambridge. His latest book is *Augustine of Hippo: His Life and Impact* (2020).

Matthew Johnston is a pastor of Lux Evangelica, a church that he helped plant in Genoa. He has served in Italy since 2013 and previously was an associate pastor in Florida. He is a graduate of The Expositors Seminary (MDiv, 2011) and the University of Glasgow (MTh, 2023), where he researched Christology in the thought of Robert Bellarmine and Francis Turretin. He is working on his PhD in historical theology at Evangelische Theologische Faculteit, Leuven.

Clay Kannard is co-pastor of the church Breccia di Roma. Clay earned a Bachelor of Science in Biblical Studies from Moody Bible Institute, a Master of Theological Studies with emphasis in Preaching and Pastoral Ministries through Midwestern Baptist Theological Seminary, and is pursuing his MTh through Union School of Theology (Rome campus). Additionally, Clay serves as the Communications Director of the Reformanda Initiative.

Reid Karr is the pastor of Chiesa Evangelica Breccia di Roma Prati and serves as the Associate Director of the Reformanda Initiative. He has served with the International Mission Board of the Southern Baptist Convention since 2009. He is also pursuing postgraduate studies at Union School of Theology (Rome campus). Reid has lived in Rome since 2009, is married and has four children.

Lauren J. Montenegro is a missionary and church planter in France. She has earned degrees in Christian Ministry from Ridley College (Melbourne, Australia) and in Philosophy: Religions and Societies from the University of Bordeaux Montaigne (France). Her Master's thesis was on the current pilgrimage trends in Lourdes. She is currently pursuing a PhD at Union School of Theology.

Feedback on this resource

We really appreciate getting feedback about our resources—not just suggestions for how to improve them, but also positive feedback and ways they can be used. We especially love to hear that the resources may have helped someone in their Christian growth.

You can send feedback to us via the 'Feedback' menu in our online store, or write to us at info@matthiasmedia.com.au.

❀matthiasmedia

Matthias Media is an evangelical publishing ministry that seeks to persuade all Christians of the truth of God's purposes in Jesus Christ as revealed in the Bible, and equip them with high-quality resources, so that by the work of the Holy Spirit they will:

- abandon their lives to the honour and service of Christ in daily holiness and decision-making
- pray constantly in Christ's name for the fruitfulness and growth of his gospel
- speak the Bible's life-changing word whenever and however they can—in the home, in the world and in the fellowship of his people.

Our wide range of resources includes Bible studies, books, training courses, tracts and children's material. To find out more, and to access samples and free downloads, visit our website:

matthiasmedia.com

How to buy our resources

1. Direct from us over the internet:
   – in the US: matthiasmedia.com
   – in Australia: matthiasmedia.com.au

2. Direct from us by phone: please visit our website for current phone contact information.

3. Through a range of outlets in various parts of the world. Visit **matthiasmedia.com/contact** for details about recommended retailers in your part of the world.

4. Trade enquiries can be addressed to:
   – in the US and Canada: sales@matthiasmedia.com
   – in Australia and the rest of the world: sales@matthiasmedia.com.au

Register at our website for our **free** regular email update to receive information about the latest new resources, **exclusive special offers**, and free articles to help you grow in your Christian life and ministry.

The Life of Faith

Peter F. Jensen

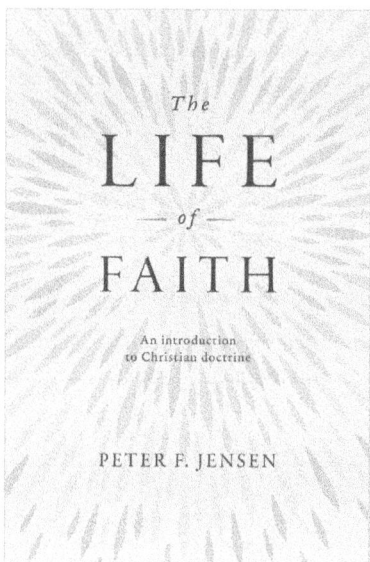

Mastered by the Word
Craig Hamilton

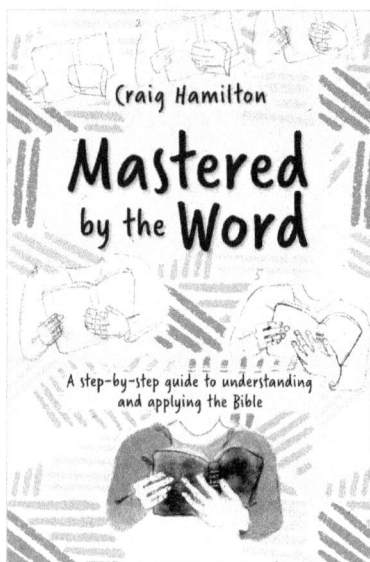

Exegesis—reading out the meaning there in the text—is a critical process that anyone teaching God's word to others can and should be thinking through, not just pastors giving sermons but also Christians leading and teaching children or in situations like growth groups. We must be mastered by the word before we wield it.

In this book, Craig Hamilton explains how to deeply and rightly read and understand the Bible by considering important issues such as context, genre, key words, Old Testament quotations, history, theology, and more. At the end of each step, he gives a masterclass on how to apply what has been covered by showing his working when exegeting the account in Mark 5 of Jesus' interaction with the demon-possessed man.

Craig is passionate about equipping every Christian to uncover all they can from a passage of Scripture and become better teachers of God's word. This step-by-step guide will take you by the hand so that what seems intimidating and only relevant for Bible college graduates becomes an intuitive process for all.

For more information or to order contact:

Matthias Media
sales@matthiasmedia.com.au
matthiasmedia.com.au

Matthias Media (USA)
sales@matthiasmedia.com
matthiasmedia.com

AVAILABLE ONLINE

Christian Essentials

Ken Noakes

CHRISTIAN
ESSENTIALS

9 key characteristics
of every follower of Jesus

KEN D NOAKES

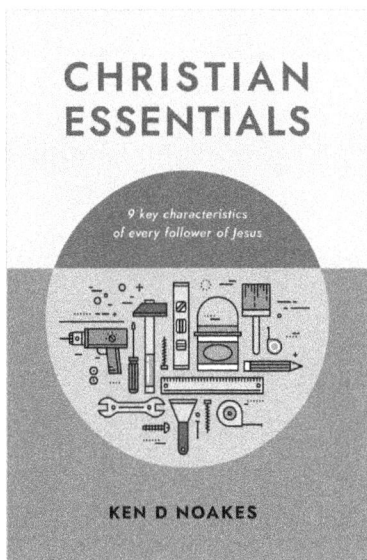

Saved by grace. Grounded in the Word. Faithful in prayer. Bold in witness. Resilient in suffering. Committed in membership. Loving in relationships. Godly in giving. Fruitful in service.

Does this sound like you? Do you wish it did?

Come with preacher and pastor Ken Noakes as he explores what it means to actively follow Jesus and "let your light shine before others". Ken provides a unique mix of imagined perspectives of the believers described in Acts, topical Bible studies, and careful teaching on these 9 Christian essentials. This book will help those who are exploring Christianity, encourage those who are new to Jesus, and grow every Christian who seeks to live according to what God desires rather than what the world values. This is a discipleship manual.